3rd Edition

COMPLETE GUIDE TO
MAKING WOODEN CLOCKS

37 Woodworking Projects for Traditional, Shaker & Contemporary Designs

JOHN A. NELSON

T0322583

FOX CHAPEL
PUBLISHING

© 2000, 2003, 2018 by John A. Nelson and Fox Chapel Publishing Company, Inc., 903 Square Street, Mount Joy, PA 17552.

Complete Guide to Making Wooden Clocks, 3rd Edition (2018) is a revised edition of *The Complete Guide to Making Wooden Clocks, 2nd Edition* (2003), published by Fox Chapel Publishing Company, Inc. Revisions include the addition of full-size pattern sheets. The patterns contained herein are copyrighted by the author. Readers may make copies of these patterns for personal use. The patterns themselves, however, are not to be duplicated for resale or distribution under any circumstances. Any such copying is a violation of copyright law.

Interior Photography: Carl Shuman, Deborah Porter-Hayes

ISBN 978-1-56523-957-9

Library of Congress Cataloging-in-Publication Data

Names: Nelson, John A., 1935-

Title: Complete guide to making wooden clocks / John A. Nelson.

Description: 3rd edition. | Mount Joy : Fox Chapel Publishing, [2018] |
  Includes index.

Identifiers: LCCN 2018008127 (print) | LCCN 2018009525 (ebook) | ISBN
  9781607655367 (e-book) | ISBN 9781565239579 (pbk.)

Subjects: LCSH: Clock and watch making--Amateurs' manuals. |
  Woodwork--Amateurs' manuals.

Classification: LCC TS545 (ebook) | LCC TS545 .N45 2018 (print) | DDC
  681.1/13--dc23

LC record available at https://lccn.loc.gov/2018008127

To learn more about the other great books from Fox Chapel Publishing, or to find a retailer near you, call toll-free
800-457-9112 or visit us at *www.FoxChapelPublishing.com*.

We are always looking for talented authors. To submit an idea, please send a brief inquiry to
acquisitions@foxchapelpublishing.com.

Printed in Singapore
First printing

Acknowledgments

Producing a comprehensive book like this requires many dedicated people. I could not have done it alone. I would like to thank the following people for their help and input: Joyce, who spent hours and hours on the computer typing, struggled with my poor penmanship, and put it all into a readable manuscript; Wesley and Alice Demarest of Sussex, New Jersey, for doing such an excellent job making all the clocks in this book—their woodworking skills are superior; and Debbie Porter-Hayes of Hancock, New Hampshire, for taking many of the wonderful photographs used in this book. To Alan Giagnocavo of Fox Chapel Publishing Company of Mount Joy, Pennsylvania, and his very dedicated staff: I want each of you to know how much I appreciate all your efforts. Your help and support really made this book.

I hope you like all our efforts!

John A. Nelson

John with the original Eli Terry Pillar and Scroll Clock.

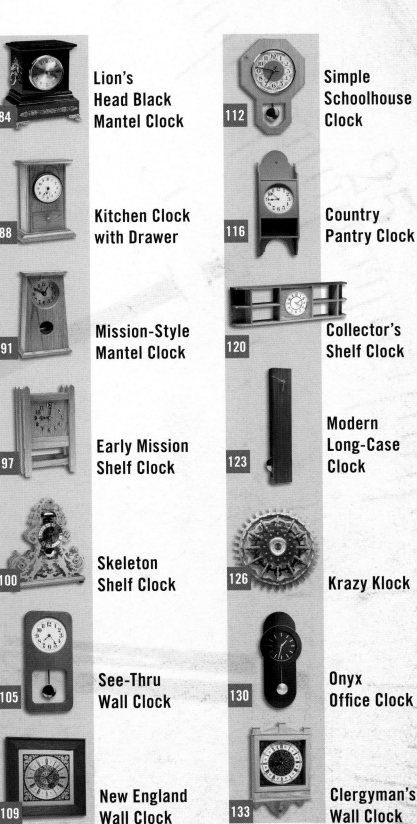
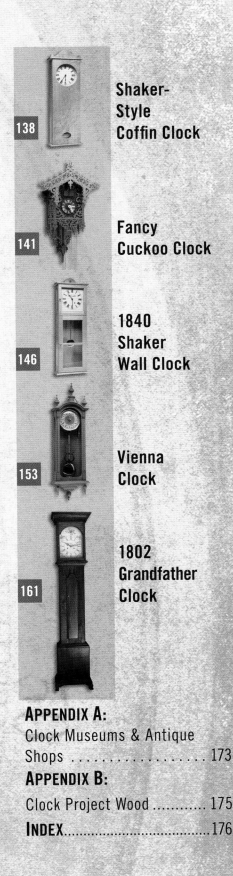

Introduction

In years past, time passed with little or no urgency. Owning a clock was an indication of prosperity rather than a commitment to punctuality.

The passing of time has always been recognized by man, and man always had a fascination with trying to measure and record that passing. At first, it was the passing of days, the waxing and waning of the moon, and the changing of the various seasons. Time was very important in early days so that people could keep track of when to plant and harvest. The actual hour and minute of the day was not particularly important.

Early sundials were invented to keep a rough track of the passing of the hours. Other simple devices such as the hourglass, indexed candles that burned at a fixed rate and water power followed. Years later, the first mechanical clocks appeared. Today clocks of all shapes and sizes help us track time right down to the millisecond.

This book is written to appeal to anyone who likes and appreciates clocks. Various kinds of clocks and designs are included to reach all woodworking levels and all interests. I am sure there is something here for everyone. I included a little history about clocks, an introduction to the latest clock parts and accessories available today, and instructions on how to make use of them and where to get them. Noted, also, is information on the National Clock and Watch Association and a few of my favorite museums located throughout the country.

I sincerely hope you will enjoy this book and that it will get you started on a clock project of your own.

In early days, town folks relied on the church or town hall clock. Owning a clock was an indication of prosperity rather than a commitment to punctuality.

CHAPTER 1

A Brief History of Clocks

The theory behind time-keeping can be traced back to the astronomer Galileo. In 1580, Galileo, who is well-known for his theories on the universe, observed a swinging lamp suspended from a cathedral ceiling by a long chain. As he studied the swinging lamp, he discovered that each swing was equal and had a natural rate of motion. Later he found this rate of motion depended upon the length of the chain. For years he thought of this, and in 1640, he designed a clock mechanism incorporating the swing of a pendulum. Unfortunately, he died before actually building his new clock design.

In 1656, Christiaan Huygens incorporated a pendulum into a clock mechanism. He found that the new clock kept excellent time. He regulated the speed of the movement, as it is done today, by moving the pendulum bob up or down: up to "speed-up" the clock and down to "slow-down" the clock.

Christiaan's invention was the boon that set man on his quest to track time with mechanical instruments.

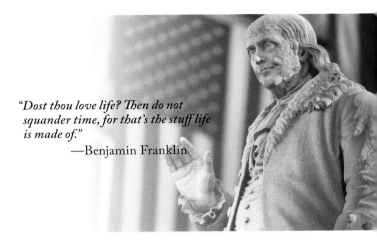

"Dost thou love life? Then do not squander time, for that's the stuff life is made of."
—Benjamin Franklin

became more accurate when the pendulum was added in 1656.

Early clock movements were mounted high above the floor on shelves because they required long pendulums and large cast-iron descending weights. These clocks were nothing more than simple mechanical works with a face and hands and were called "wags-on-the-wall." Long-case clocks, or tall-case clocks, actually evolved from the early wags-on-the-wall clocks. They were nothing more than wooden cases added to hide the unsightly weights and cast-iron pendulums.

EARLY MECHANICAL CLOCKS

Early mechanical clocks, probably developed by monks from central Europe in the last half of the thirteen century, did not have pendulums. Neither did they have dials or hands. They told time only by striking a bell on the hour. These early clocks were very large and were made of heavy iron frames and gears forged by local blacksmiths. Most were placed in church belfries to make use of existing church bells.

Small domestic clocks with faces and dials started to appear by the first half of the fifteenth century. By 1630, a weight-driven lantern clock became popular in the homes of the very wealthy. These early clocks were made by local gunsmiths or locksmiths. Clocks

JOHN HARRISON (1693–1776)

Little is known about this man, the one person who, I think, did the most for clock- making. John was an English clockmaker, a mechanical genius, who devoted his life to clock-making. He accomplished what Isaac Newton, known for his theories on gravity, said was impossible.

John Harrison was born March 24, 1693, in the English county of Yorkshire. John learned woodworking from his father, but taught himself how to build a clock. He made his first clock in 1713 at the age of 19. It was made almost entirely of wood with oak wheels (gears). In 1722 he constructed a tower clock for Brocklesby Park. That clock has been running continuously for over 270 years.

One year later, on July 8, 1714, England offered £20,000 (approximately 12 million dollars) to anyone whose method proved successful in measuring longitude. Such a device was desperately needed by

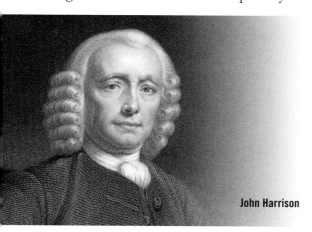

John Harrison

navigators of sailing vessels. Sailors during this time were literally lost at sea as soon as they lost sight of land. One man, John Harrison, felt longitude could be measured with a clock.

During the summer of 1730, John started work on a clock that would keep precise time at sea—something no one had yet been able to do with a clock. In five years he had his first model, H-1. It weighted 75 pounds and was four feet tall, four feet wide and four feet long. To prove his theory, John built H-2, H-3 and H-4.

His method of locating longitude by time was finally accepted and he won the prize. It took him over 40 years. Today, his perfect timekeeper is known as a chronometer.

CLOCKS IN THE COLONIES

In the early 1600s, clocks were brought to the colonies by wealthy colonists. Clocks were found only in the finest of homes. Most people of that time had to rely on the church clock on the town common for the time of day.

Most early clockmakers were not skilled in woodworking, so they turned to woodworkers to make the cases for them. These early woodworkers employed the same techniques used on furniture of the day. In 1683, immigrant William Davis claimed to be a "complete" clockmaker. He is considered to be the first clockmaker in the new colony.

Great horological artisans immigrated to the New World by 1799. Most of these early artisans settled in populous centers such as Boston, Philadelphia, New York, Charleston, Baltimore and New Haven.

Clock-making grew in all areas of the eastern part of the colonies. The earliest and most famous clockmakers

Most Early American clocks had wooden gears, as brass was very expensive and hard to obtain.

from Philadelphia were Samuel Bispam, Abel Cottey and Peter Stretch. The most famous clockmaker was Philadelphia's David Rittenhouse. David succeeded Benjamin Franklin as president of the American Philosophical Society and later became Director of the United States Mint.

Nineteenth Century Grandfather Clocks

Inexpensive tall-case clocks were made in quantity and became more affordable after 1800. The clock-making industry spread to the northeastern states. In Massachusetts, Benjamin and Ephram Willard became famous for their exceptionally beautiful long-case clocks. In Connecticut, mass-produced long-case clocks were developed by Eli Terry.

In early days, almost all clock cases were made by local cabinetmakers. A firm that specialized in clock works fashioned the wood or bronze works. Cabinetmakers engraved or painted their names on the dial faces, thereby taking claim for the completed clocks.

With the advent of the Industrial Revolution, regular factory working hours and the introduction of train schedules, standardized timekeeping became a necessity. Clock-making moved to the forefront.

Wooden movements were abandoned in 1840 and 30-hour brass movements became popular. They were easy to make and inexpensive. Spring-powered movements were developed soon after. A variety of totally new and smaller clock cases appeared on the market.

Nineteenth-Century Manufacturers

Clock manufacturers were mostly individual clockmakers of family-owned companies. After 1840 however, Chauncy Jerome built the largest clock factory in the United States. He started shipping clocks all over the world. The Jerome Clock Company motivated the organization of the Ansonia Clock Company and the Waterbury Clock Company. These three companies, along with Seth Thomas Company, the E. N. Welch Company, the Ingraham Clock Company, and the Gilbert Clock Company, became the major producers of clocks in the nineteenth century. There were over 30 clock factories in this country by 1851. From 1840 up to 1890, millions of clocks were produced in this country, but unfortunately, very few still exist intact today.

Elias Ingraham

Elias was born in 1805 in Marlborough, Connecticut. He served a 5-year apprenticeship in cabinetmaking in the early 1820s. By 1828, at the age of 23, Elias was designing and building clock cases for George Mitchell. When he was 25 years old, he worked for the Chauncey and Lawson Ives Clock Company, which was still designing and building clock cases.

Elias formed a new company with his brother Andrew in 1852 called the E. and A. Ingraham and Company, but 4 years later, it went bankrupt. A year later he formed his own company with his son, Edward. Changing the name to E. Ingraham and Company, the business began manufacturing clock cases. By 1862, his then successful company manufactured its own movements, as well.

Throughout his lifetime, Elias was granted many clock case design patents. He died in 1885, but the company he started continued. Elias was perhaps the greatest clock case designer ever, and his clock designs are still being copied and produced today.

Marshall and Adams Clock Factory, Seneca Falls, New York, circa 1856.

CLOCK-MAKING IN THE TWENTIETH CENTURY

Most of the clockmakers who produced thousands of clocks during the 1800s failed in the twentieth century. During the stock market crash of 1929, the Ansonia Clock Company moved its operation to Russia, and the Seth Thomas Clock Company became a part of the General Time Instrument Company. From 1940 to the present, the Sessions Clock Company and the New Haven Clock Company were founded. Of the original giants of the clock industry, only three exist today: Seth Thomas is now a division of Talley Industries, the Ingraham Clock Company is now a division of McGraw-Edison, and Gilbert Clock Company has been replaced by the Sparta Corporation.

Today there are no spring-powered movements or clocks currently produced in this country. Some of the quartz movements found in today's clocks are produced here, but most are made abroad.

Waterbury Clock Company

The Waterbury Clock Company started as the Benedict and Burnham Brass Manufacturing Company and, in 1850, became part of Jerome Company. With only $60,000, the Waterbury Clock Company was formed in Waterbury, Connecticut in 1857. It was a major maker of clocks in the United States from 1857 to 1944.

CHAPTER 2

America's Popular Clocks

CLOCK CLASSIFICATIONS AND TYPES

Like many antiques, clocks are classified by their overall style. There are five overall styles of clocks: Colonial, Empire, Victorian, Modern, and Contemporary.

- *Colonial* — built up to 1800; tall-case and wags-on-the wall clocks

- *Empire* — 1800–1840; mostly wooden movements; shelf clocks and tall-case clocks; 30-hour or 8-day movements

- *Victorian* — 1840–1890; the period of greatest production of clocks and the greatest variety of models; advent of the 30-hour brass movement and the spring-powered movement

- *Modern* — 1890–1940; a period of change from mechanical movements to clocks with synchronous electric motors

- *Contemporary* — World War II–present; great changes occur, from the development of electric motors to clocks with very accurate electronic (quartz) movements

Clocks are further categorized by types. There are three primary types of clocks: tall-case, wall and shelf.

TALL CLOCKS

The grandfather clock, once called the long clock, tallcase clock or even coffin clock, has always been particularly popular. The term "grandfather clock" came from a song of the same name written by Henry Clay in 1876.

The original tall-case clock is said to have been developed in London around 1650. The earliest tall-case clock built in America was made by Abel Cottey around 1720. Under the direction of Connecticut clockmaker Eli Terry, the tall-case clock was also the first household piece to be successfully mass-produced in America. Through the years, it has been known as an excellent timekeeper.

In early America, most grandfather clocks were made with flat tops. By 1740, however, during the Queen Anne period, clocks were made with round tops. The Chippendale style then became popular, followed by the most popular design, the Federal "swan-neck" top. These cases reflected the styles of the period. Other styles included Sheraton and Hepplewhite.

A modern grandfather clock. (Photo used with permission of the American Clock Company.)

As glass was very expensive in those days, the front doors on grandfather clocks were made from solid wood. The solid door also hid the 42-inch-long pendulum and cast-iron weights, which were very crudely constructed.

Tall-case clock cases consist of the base, waist and hood. Some original designs included feet, waist and door columns, hood fretwork and finials. Cases were constructed from many kinds of woods, although local hardwoods such as maple, cherry, walnut and mahogany were common. Other, lower-cost clocks were made of pine. A painted grain was added to simulate the more desired and more expensive hardwood.

Many cases were very elegant and beautiful; others were extremely crude. At the height of their popularity, many tallcase clocks were over nine feet tall. Today, most range from six feet to seven feet, six inches in height. Cases shorter than six feet are considered grandmother clocks.

WALL CLOCKS

The wall clock was the first truly American clock made in the colonies. The most popular of all wall clocks was the small-case, elegant hanging timepiece called the "patent time-piece." Later, it was called the banjo clock. It was made by Simon Willard of Massachusetts in the 1820s, and it satisfied the American fantasies of luxury and refinement of the day.

Craftsman from New Hampshire and Connecticut added a looking glass to the wall clock, thereby adding another function to the wall clock. Aaron Willard and Joseph Ives were the first clockmakers to produce many mirrored wall clocks.

SHELF CLOCKS

The Willards of Massachusetts designed and built thevery famous first Massachusetts shelf clocks. They were usually made to order and very expensive. Affordable shelf clocks came into existence after 1807. Eli Terry received an order to build 4,000 wooden-geared movements. It took him over two years to complete the order, but his experiments helped him develop the first true mass-production factory andmadeshelf clocks available to everyone. The most fashionable wall clocks were replaced by cheaper shelf clocks in 1850 or so.

MAJOR MILESTONES IN AMERICAN CLOCK-MAKING

Clock-making in America can be traced back to just prior to the American Revolution. Over the past two hundred years, various styles of clocks have become popular. These clocks were replaced by other styles as years past.

PILLAR AND SCROLL CLOCK

Eli Terry is referred to as the father of American clock manufacturing. He was born in 1772, in South Windsor, Connecticut, just before the American Revolution.

In 1814, Terry developed what I feel is the most beautiful shelf clock ever built and manufactured in the United States. It was the very popular pillar and scroll shelf clock.

The original pillar and scroll varied slightly in design from 1814 to 1822. There were five slightly different wooden movements used during that time, also.

Most of the original pillar and scroll clocks made were powered by 30-hour weight-driven, key-wound, wooden geared movements. A very few had the new improved 8-day wooden movements.

The one photographed is one of the original designs. It was made about 1820 by Eli Terry and Sons of Plymouth, Connecticut, and has a 30-hour, weight-driven, wooden movement. This clock also has an original paper that gives running instructions and the maker's name and address.

For years, many other clock companies copied the pillar and scroll clock design. Today, originals of these clocks are very expensive.

Chauncy Jerome, a carpenter working for Eli Terry at the time, is the person who actually made the first pillar and scroll clock case, although Eli Terry has always been credited with the clock.

Early Eli Terry Pillar and Scroll Clock, circa 1830. Note the reverse painting on the lower section of glass. The colors were laid down in reverse order on the back of the glass.

COLUMN AND SPLAT CLOCK

In 1828, George Mitchell hired a cabinetmaker by the name of Elias Ingraham to develop a case design in order to compete with the pillar and scroll clock. Within a year, Elias created the column and splat clock. This new clock design featured columns, lion's-paw feet and a patriotic eagle splat top. (The term "splat" refers to the decorator piece at the top of the clock case.) A painting on the door glass was done with a technique called reverse painting. The painting was actually done on the inside of the glass door. Colors were laid down in a reverse order so that the painting

Early column and splat clock, circa 1840. The "splat" is the top trim piece.

appeared normal when viewed from the opposite side of the glass.

The column and splat clock was copied by many clockmakers of the day. To save money, some companies added a looking glass in the door in place of the reverse painting. Eli Terry developed a model of his own that he called the "transitional model," but his version was based on his original pillar and scroll design.

In time, the pillar and scroll clock was replaced by the newer clock design. Column and splat clocks were very popular from 1829 to 1845, and there were over nineteen clockmakers producing this model.

COLUMN CLOCK

During the Victorian period, the new popular clock was the column clock. Note the classical influence and empire base and gilded columns. These column clocks were made in Connecticut, New York and Massachusetts as early as 1824 and as late as 1885. They reflect the formal styles of popular furniture of the day. Column clocks were made with two or even three doors and some had both a looking glass and reversed painting.

Column clocks were more expensive than other shelf clocks of the day. Some of them had the somewhat new and improved 8-day, spring-driven brass movements.

These clocks usually had white-painted-tin dial faces. Some had openings in the center of the dial faces so the brass movements could be seen. This also allowed the oiling of the verge and escapement wheel.

Column clock from the Victorian period, circa 1875.

OGEE CLOCK

There is something about the ogee clock that everyone likes. Many clock collectors started their collections with an ogee. I once went to an auction and watched one person buy five of them. He wasn't a collector or dealer—he simply liked them!

The ogee name is derived from the name of the simple, curved molding used in the clock's construction. This clock is nothing more than a rectangular box with a door with an ogee molding. It has simple, weight-driven brass works that just about anyone can take apart and repair. It is among the simplest of clocks made.

These simple clocks were made as early as 1827. It is not know who designed the ogee clock, though many speculate it was Chauncey Jerome. They were moderately priced clocks and were popular from 1830 to 1859.

Simple ogee clock with mirrored door.

The very first ogee clocks had wooden geared movements, but overall, most had simple 30-hour, weight-driven brass movements. Some ogee clocks had a mirror in the door; more expensive models had reversed paintings on the door. Ogee clocks came in all sizes, from the very small (4 inches deep, 11½ inches wide and 18 inches high) to the very large model (5½ inches deep, 18 inches wide and 31 inches high). The ogee on page nine is a standard size (4½ inches deep, 15½ inches wide and 25¾ inches high).

Some ogee clocks have a flat molding in place of the ogee molding and are referred to as "beveled-case clocks" or "flat ogee clocks."

CALENDAR CLOCK

Clockmakers developed a timepiece in 1850 that provided the hour of the day, day of the week, day of the month, and month of the year. Some models even indicated the phase of the moon, as well as high and low tides. Every 24 hours, at midnight, a pin on a gear turned once, putting the calendar mechanism into operation. Calendar clocks were adapted into the schoolhouse clock style.

The calendar clock gave its owner a method of long-range planning. We rely today on desk calendars, quartz watches, electric clocks, radios or television. Remember, in 1870 and before the adoption of standard time, this calendar information was not readily available to everyone.

Calendar clocks provided the hour of the day, day of the week, day of the month and month of the year.

The Ithaca Clock Company, the Ansonia Brass and Copper Company and the Waterbury Clock Company started making their own calendar clocks in 1880. These calendar clocks were very popular until 1910. Today, calendar clocks are sought after by almost all clock collectors.

This model at the upper left was manufactured by Seth Thomas and patented on December 18, 1875. It is a pedimented, partial-octagon clock in the Victorian style with some Gothic influence. This model counts the hours, on the hour, and rings once every half hour.

STEEPLE CLOCK

The Connecticut clockmaker, Elias Ingraham, who designed the column and splat clock, was also a skilled cabinetmaker. He designed and produced many fine clock cases of the day.

In 1845, he designed an unusual "sharp," gothic clock case that featured church-like spires. Today it is called the steeple clock.

The steeple clock is one of the most popular clock models ever made. It is still being reproduced today. In

A popular Gothic design is the steeple clock.

its day, this clock was copied by most all existing clock companies.

Most early steeple clocks contained a 30-hour brass movement. Eight-day movement models are somewhat rare, cost much more and are more desirable. Steeple clocks range in height from 10½ inches to 23 inches.

Cottage clocks were popular from 1865 to 1895.

COTTAGE CLOCK

Cottage clocks are a simple, pleasant form of the Connecticut shelf clock. The cottage clocks were popular during the Victorian age and replaced the somewhat larger, more expensive box clocks of the day.

Cottage clocks are very small. Each clock was usually less than 12 inches high. Most models had simple 30-hour movements; some even had alarms.

Cottage clocks were made in great volume from 1865 through 1895. Many models had decorated doors.

Today, cottage clocks are still fairly popular. Unfortunately, they are of limited value because of their 30-hour movement.

FIGURE EIGHT CLOCK

The figure eight clock is shaped like a number eight. The top circle, which houses the clock face, is usually larger than the bottom circle. It is another early example of Elias Ingraham's work. He patented this design around 1862 and named it the "ionic" wall clock.

Elias hired Anson Atwood to set up and run a movement manufacturing division of the Ingraham Company. This allowed the company to manufacture both the movement and the case. Before this time, Elias had purchased movements from Noah Pomeroy and the Waterbury Brass Company.

The figure eight clock was the forerunner of the popular schoolhouse clock, developed in 1875 by the Ansonia Clock Company.

The figure eight clock is the forerunner of the popular schoolhouse clock.

BANJO CLOCK

The Willard family of Massachusetts designed and built many beautiful clocks.

In 1795, Simon designed a totally new wall clock, which he called the "improved time-piece." He patented it in 1802, and it was an instant success with the burgeoning middle class. The case is shaped like a banjo. Famous naval battles were painted on the bottom glass, and the top glass panel was gold-gilded with a matching design. Some banjo clocks had brass side brackets. Today, clocks built by Benjamin, Simon, Ephram and Aaron Willard demand top dollar, if you can find one for sale. Simon Willard learned clockmaking from his older brother, Benjamin, and settled in Roxbury, Massachusetts, right after the Revolutionary War.

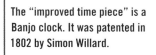

The "improved time piece" is a Banjo clock. It was patented in 1802 by Simon Willard.

Schoolhouse Clock

For many years, schoolhouse clocks were hung on the wall next to Gilbert Stuart's framed painting of George Washington in school rooms all over the country. I hate to date myself, but I can vividly remember those days myself. Unfortunately, those wonderful old clocks have been replaced today by "cold" high-tech electronic clocks.

In 1875, the Ansonia Clock Company developed a very popular clock, the Model-A long drop octagon clock—a forerunner of the schoolhouse clock. This model was an instant success and was sold throughout the entire world almost overnight.

The long drop octagon clock was shortened and became what we recognize as a schoolhouse clock.

Schoolhouse clocks were sold from 1875 to 1910, but they didn't go out of style until the 1950s. The clocks were eventually made in all sizes by almost all major clock companies. Countries such as China and Korea also made schoolhouse clocks in great quantities. Today many of the so-called antique schoolhouse clocks you find in antique shops are actually Korean, not American antiques. Care should be taken in buying an old school house clock.

Schoolhouse clocks were popular from 1875 to 1910.

The Ansonia Clock Company made excellent, high-quality movements, but due to the Great Depression, it went out of business in 1929. What was left of the company was moved to Russia, but it never really regained the success it had achieved in the United States.

Regulator Clock

The term "Regulator" generally refers to a very precise, plain-cased clock with a long pendulum and no bell chimes to sound the hour. Seth Thomas' original and famous Regulator No. 2 wall clock was very popular in America from 1870 to 1920. Almost every office, church or bank of any size at all had a Regulator No. 2 hanging on the wall.

Regulator No. 2 was made of oak (sometimes walnut), with an 8-day, high-quality, weight-driven movement. The movement was mounted on a heavy cast-iron support, which is a little unusual for most American clocks. The design changed very little throughout all the years of manufacturing. An exact copy of this movement with the cast-iron support can be still purchased today.

Regulator Clock No. 2 was one of America's favorite office clocks. Popular from 1870 to 1920, most were made of oak, but a few were made of walnut.

GINGERBREAD CLOCK

The most common and, until recently, the least liked clock from the Victorian age is the gingerbread clock. When first introduced in 1800, it was called the "Kitchen Clock." The gingerbread clock was very popular in the Victorian homes of the middle and lower classes. They were in vogue until 1900. Later models used pressed molded wings and tops. These were stamped out of wood by the tens of thousands. Gingerbread clocks were made in all shapes and sizes—most not very attractive at all. These clocks were made of oak or walnut. Today, original gingerbread clocks are gaining in popularity again, and their cost is rising yearly.

Gingerbread clocks had striking movements on a bell for each hour and single strikes for the half hour. An accessory was an obnoxious alarm that would drive you out of bed very quickly—like it or not!

I think the only elegant gingerbread clock ever made was the Patti Parlor walnut model. It was manufactured by G.N. Welch Manufacturing Company in 1887, and today it is sought after by many clock collectors.

A clock design from the Victorian age is the gingerbread clock. Most were made of oak.

MISSION CLOCK

The Mission clocks were developed at the end of the Victorian era and replaced the gingerbread models. They were an effort to return to a simple and honest design and were popular from 1900 until 1930.

Mission clocks were usually made of oak, as was most Mission furniture of the time. The clocks were made to convey the functionalist designers' sense of moral commitment or "mission" to create a simple and pure design. They were made as tall-case clocks, wall clocks and mantel clocks.

Mision clocks replaced the gingerbread clocks.

Black Mantel Clock

American clock companies developed a totally new small black mantel clock in 1870. These clocks were well-made and inexpensive; they were manufactured using the latest clock technology of the day and had all the new and improved features.

Black mantel clocks were nothing more than a rectangular, wooden, black-painted box with either Doric or Ionic columns. Many of these clocks have lion heads mounted on the sides and brass, claw-like feet on the bottom.

Black mantel clocks were well made and used excellent, dependable movements.

Real marble was incorporated into the design of some of the black mantel clocks during the Victorian era. Most clockmakers, used a painted marble veneer, called admantine, over wood. Black mantel clocks were popular for over 40 years, from 1880 to 1920, but were eventually replaced by the new model Tambour clock.

William Gilbert Welch, along with all major clock manufacturing companies of the day, made black mantel clocks in very large quantities. They were made in all kinds of shapes and sizes, with all kinds of column combinations and decorations. Today you can still find many of these clocks in antique shops throughout the country. Some are very pretty; many were not pretty at all.

Until recently, black mantel clocks were not very popular, but today they are gaining more and more interest from collectors. Their movements are of the highest quality of the day, keep excellent time, and will run for another 100 years or more. These black clocks are the "sleepers" of the antique world. I feel in a few years they will be in demand and their prices will increase dramatically.

Tambour Clock

The Tambour clock replaced the black mantel clocks around 1908. Tambour clocks are sometimes referred to as "humpback" clocks. They had their heyday from 1920 to 1930 but were still popular up to 1950. The clock is shaped like a tambourine drum, hence the name "Tambour." These clocks are not antiques as most of them are not over one hundred years old, yet.

Experts estimate that over a million Tambour clocks have been made. Most contain either an 8-day or 30-day movement. Today they are referred to simply as mantel clocks and are still being made, though most Tambour clocks manufactured today incorporate the new quartz movement.

The Tambour clock is sometimes called the "Humpback" clock. They had their heyday from 1920 to 1930. They were the last mass-produced clock and the last clock with mechanical movements made in this country.

CONCLUSION

Many clocks of foreign design, including the Vienna wall clock and the Black Forest cuckoo clock, have also been popular in America. Some are produced here in the United States. However, the Tambour clock is really the last vastly popular American model to be developed. No other clock model has since been produced to take its place in the United States.

A Cuckoo clock. (Photo used with permission of the American Clock Co.)

A Vienna Regulator clock. (Photo used with permission of the American Clock Co.)

Dates of Operation for Major American Clock Manufacturers

E. Ingraham & Co.
1861-1958

Elias Ingraham & Co.
1857-1860

E.N. Welch Mfg. Co.
1864-1903

F. Kroeber (& Co.)
1863-1887

F. Kroeber Clock Co.
1887-1904

Gilbert Mfg. Co.
1866-1871

New Haven Clock Co.
1853-c.1965

Sessions Clock Co.
1903-1956

Seth Thomas
1813-1853

Seth Thomas Clock Co.
(Plymouth Hollow, CT)
1853-1865

Seth Thomas Clock
Co. (Thomaston, CT)
1866-1930

Seth Thomas Div.
of General Time
1930-present

Waterbury Clock Co.
1857-1944

William L. Gilbert Clock
Co. 1871-1934

William L. Gilbert Clock
Corp. 1934-1957

W.L. Gilbert & Co.
1845-1848 and 1851-1866

CHAPTER 3

Clock Components

If you spend a lot of time making a clock—and you will—you do not want to skimp and use inexpensive, poorly made components. Today, there are all kinds of clock-related components available. These wonderful components add that "finished," professional look. Before starting any clock making project, locate and contact various companies that sell clock parts and accessories for their catalogs. A few of their products are illustrated here to give you an idea of some of the components that are available.

Ordering Parts

Parts vary slightly from vendor to vendor. A six-inch-diameter dial face from one vendor might measure 6¼ inches in diameter from another vendor. It is important that you order the hardware and movement before starting a clock project so that you can make minor adjustments for slight differences in purchased parts. Also check that the movement's dimensions are correct. If a pendulum is used, check that the pendulum length is correct and that it will swing properly in the given space. Check that the length of the center hand shaft is long enough, but not too long, as the tip of the center hand shaft must not touch the glass on the dial face (if glass is used).

If you use a quartz movement you should not have any problems at all, except for the length of the center shaft. Unlike a spring-powered movement, the pendulum length on a quartz movement has no effect on the operation of the movement like a spring-powered movement does, so the pendulum can be cut to any length as necessary.

The brass dial bezel diameter also has a tendency to vary slightly from vendor to vendor, so you should

check these as well before starting a project. If possible, try to get dial face bezels with the glass and dial already assembled.

Choosing a Clock Movement

Quartz movements are rather simple to install and instructions are usually included. The mechanical brass movements usually do not include instructions, so you should have a basic knowledge of how to adjust and set up these movements.

Whether purchasing a quartz or mechanical movement, you must consider the following:

Price: Avoid the least expensive movements.

Length of center shaft: Quartz movements are usually attached to the dial face through the center hole. Be sure to double-check this length.

Note: Because the quartz movement is attached through the dial face, you must purchase a movement with the correct center shaft length. A thin dial requires a short center shaft. A thick dial requires a long center shaft. Allow enough length for the nut and washer. Be sure the center shaft is not too long so that it hits the glass door (if used).

Pendulum length: The pendulum (if one is required) does not make the quartz movement run; it is for appearance only. The length of the pendulum is usually considered the length from the center of the dial to the center of the pendulum bob; on quartz movements, it is measured from the center of the dial to the tip of the pendulum bob. Watch that the pendulum does not hit the sides of the case when it swings.

Chimes: Check that space is available to accommodate chimes if they are required.

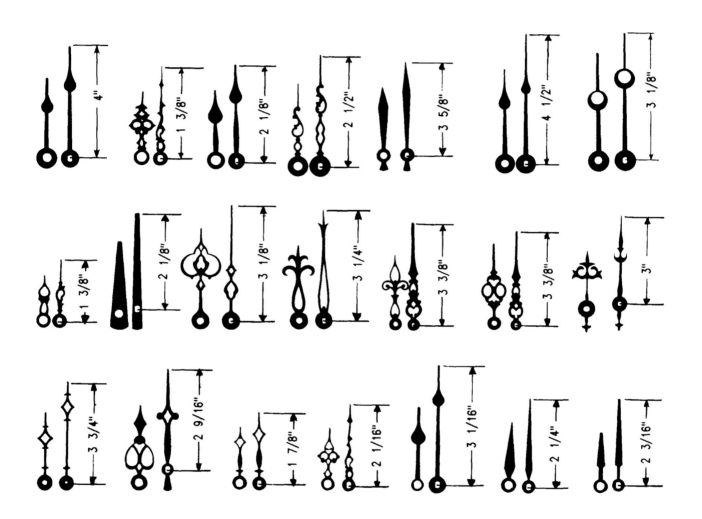

GRANDFATHER CLOCKS

Today, large clocks such as Grandfather clocks and large wall clocks take mechanical movements very easily. The Kieninger cable-driven 9-tube movement is one of the finest large movements made and available today.

CLOCK KITS

There are many wonderful clock kits for those who would love to build a clock but do not have all the woodworking tools to make all the pieces. These kits are a lot of fun to make. They are perfect for those who want a head start.

MECHANICAL MOVEMENTS

In years past, brass mechanical movements were always used to power clocks. Today brass mechanical movements are still available and will give you the real ticking effect. Brass movements require a lot of work to fit them into a clock, and the movements must be wound once a week or once a month, however, the effort is well worth the finished result.

Some brass movements are designed for quick and easy installation. Armor Crafts has a beautiful bim-bam chime unit that is complete and very simple to install.

ELECTRIC MOVEMENTS

Electric movements are also available. They are easy to install and can be used in new clocks or to repair worn electric movements in old clocks.

Quartz Gear Movements

This is an example of a quartz-powered movement with gears showing. It makes a great combination of quartz power with the look of mechanical gears.

Another quartz/gear movement is the 400-day anniversary movement. You can build a clock around this movement. It even comes with a glass dome if you wish.

Quartz Weight-Driven Movement

Quartz weight-driven movements are also available. In a quartz movement such as this one, the weights are false but look real. You can design and build a clock around this movement.

Fit-ups or Insert Movements

One of the easiest movements to use is the fit-up movement. It comes complete with movement, dial face, bezel and hands—one simple-to-use unit. You have to cut a round hole to mount these clocks.

Some fit-ups come with photos on the face, which add a lot to your clock with no extra work for you.

There are even multi-functional units available with time, day, date and moon phase all built in. These make your clock even more helpful.

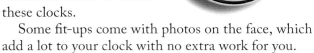

Simple Quartz Movements

Simple quartz movements are the most popular movements and have the most flexibility. They come with and without pendulums and with or without chimes or bells. In choosing a simple quartz movement, be sure to check the shaft length. Check how thick the dial face is and order a shaft length slightly longer than the thickness of the dial face.

Simple quartz movements can be purchased in extra-long 31-inch pendulum lengths so that they can be used in grandfather clocks.

An interesting option for a special quartz movement is a moonphase dial.

Dial Faces

If you use a simple quartz movement, a dial face and hands must be used with it. Dial faces come in plain, thick paper, brass or wood. Some come with brass bezel, hinge and glass ready to mount.

Faces come with brass trim similar to the dial faces used in regular or Vienna clocks. These give a formal flair to most any clock.

Very fancy, beautiful grandfather clock dials are also available. They come with raised corners and numbers. Some come with a moon phase dial.

Brass Components

High-quality components add a lot to any project. Heavy solid-brass hinges are a must on any quality clock project.

Brass screws always look good. Keep in mind they are soft and break very easily. It is a good idea to use a steel screw first, then remove it and add the brass screws. (I also use wax from a candle to lubricate brass screws.)

Brass hangers always add "class" to any project. Attach them with brass screws or tacks. You might want to polish the hanger before attaching it to the clock.

Antique brass corners are available for dial faces or trim pieces.

High-quality brass finials and eagles give an expensive, finished look. People will admire and appreciate these components for years to come.

Desk Accessories

Pencil and pen sets can be used with desk clocks.

CHAPTER 4

Making Your Own Clock

In general, clockmaking follows the same steps. Those steps are outlined later in this chapter when we show you how to make a coffin clock.

BEFORE YOU BEGIN

Everyone has different woodworking tools and different skill levels. Take your time and enjoy yourself when you make your clock. If you need to learn more about a tool or hone your woodworking skills in a certain area, do that before you start your clock project.

As with any woodworking project, carefully study the drawings before starting so you know exactly how the clock is assembled and how each individual part is made. Try to go through each process step-by-step in your mind so you will know how to make each part with the tools and equipment available to you. As you proceed, keep all cuts square and all tool edges sharp.

TOOLS

Making the clocks from the plans in this book requires very few tools. Basic hand tools will be needed, along with the following power tools:

- Table saw or radial-arm saw

- Router and/or shaper

- Jigsaw or scroll saw

- Lathe (for 1 or 2 clocks only)

- Sander planer (optional, but handy)

Caution: Always utilize extreme caution when using any tool and maintain safe practices to avoid accidents. Be sure to wear eye and ear protection.

USING THE DRAWINGS

Any information specific to the 37 clock projects in this book is noted with the plans for that particular project.

Two or three views are provided for each clock project: a **front view, a right side view and/or a top view.**

The front view is always the most important view and should be your starting point. As space allows, the right-side view is located directly to the right of the front view; the top view is located directly above the front view. All features in the front view are transferred directly to the right-side view and the top view.

Dashed lines on the drawing indicate a hidden surface of a feature within the object. Think of these hidden lines as X-rays showing what the inside of the clock looks like.

A thin line made up of short and long dashes is the **centerline (C/L)**. It indicates the exact center of the clock or part.

Important: All drawings are fully dimensioned. The actual required size is called-off and is the distance between the tips of the arrowheads.

Section views are sometimes used to further illustrate a particular feature of the clock, to illustrate how an area is assembled, or to show the shape or profile of a molding. On the drawing, two arrows are drawn with an A or a B at the tips of the arrows. The section view shows what the piece would look like if the clock were cut in two at the arrows. This view will be listed as "View at A–A" or "View at B–B."

Study the drawings very carefully. Some parts must be made in a right-hand and left-hand pair. The side of a clock is a good example: Both sides of the clock are the same, but you must make a right side and a left side.

In addition to the regular views, most projects have an exploded view that illustrates how the clock parts fit together. Again, be sure you fully understand how the clock is assembled before you start any work.

PARTS LIST

Most clocks have a complete parts list specifying every part used in the clock. On the parts list, the number to the left of the part is the same number noted on the drawing. Each part can be easily found and copied by matching the numbers.

Important: All efforts have been made to ensure that the dimensions of each part are correct; however, it is always best to recheck each part with its mate by dry-fitting all of the parts as you proceed.

MATERIALS

A clock is the focal point of any room. In addition to being a functional object, a clock is also a decoration.

Wes and Alice Demarest, who cut the clocks featured in this book, went out of their way to use different kinds of wood and various combinations to illustrate what unique and unusual woods look like on the project clocks. (See Appendix B.) It doesn't take any more time to make a project out of a plain piece of pine than it does to make it from an interesting piece of purpleheart or zebra wood.

The cost of using an unusual wood is a little more—in fact it could be five times more—but most projects in this book do not use very much material, so the actual cost is not excessive. Your decision to choose an unusual, highly grained, interesting wood will guarantee that your clock will be admired for years to come.

ADHESIVES

We used Titebond® wood glue for both hardwood and softwood clocks in this book. The surfaces need to be clean and dry in order for the adhesive to work properly. Dry fit all the pieces and trim them if necessary before gluing; joints should fit snugly. To ensure a good bond, spread the glue and clamp the pieces in place for thirty minutes or more. Let the glue dry for another twenty-four hours. Be sure not to get glue on the wood surfaces.

For glass, plastic or metal use a product called E-6000®. This is an adhesive used in industry and is an exceptional craft adhesive for all kinds of applications. Apply E-6000® to both surfaces. Allow the pieces to bond for ten minutes or so, then press the surfaces together. Let the pieces dry for five or six hours before handling. A 48-hour period is required for E-6000® to dry to full strength.

FINISHING INSTRUCTIONS

After completing your clock, you are now ready to finish it. This is the most important part of clockmaking and should not be rushed. Remember, the clock you make will be seen for years to come. Beautiful wood, good hardware and perfect joints can not overcome a poor finish; that alone will ruin your project.

PREPARING

Before applying any stain, you must first prepare the wood. The following preliminaries are imperative to a quality finish.

- All joints should be checked for tight fits. If necessary, apply water putty to all joints, allowing ample time for drying. Set and fill nail heads with water putty.

- Sand the clock all over in the direction of the wood grain. If you are sanding by hand, use a sanding block and keep all of the clock's corners sharp. Sand all over using 100-grit paper. Resand with

120-grit paper. If necessary, sand a final time with 180-grit paper. Take care not to round the edges.

- If you do need or want any of the edges rounded, use 120-grit paper, then 180-grit paper to round the edges.

- Carefully check that all surfaces are smooth, dry and dust-free before proceeding.

STAINING

There are two major kinds of stain: water stains and oil stains.

Water stains are purchased in powder form and mixed as needed by dissolving the powder in hot water. Water stains have a tendency to raise the grain of the wood. If you use a water stain, sand the clock lightly with fine paper after the stain dries.

Oil stains are made from pigments ground in linseed oil. They do not raise the grain.

Before you begin, test the stain on a scrap piece of the same kind of lumber you plan to use to make certain you have the correct color.

When applying stain, wipe or brush on the stain as quickly and as evenly as possible to avoid overlapping streaks. If you want a darker finish, apply more than one coat of stain. Try not to apply too much stain on the end grain.

Allow the piece to dry in a dust-free area for at least 24 hours.

FILLERS

Use a paste filler for porous wood such as oak or mahogany to ensure a smooth finish. Purchase paste filler slightly darker than the color of the wood; the wood you use will darken with age.

Before using paste filler, thin it with turpentine so it can be applied with a brush. Use a stiff brush and work in the direction of the grain to fill the pores. After 15 or 20 minutes, wipe off the excess with a piece of burlap pulled gently across the grain. Take care to leave filler in the pores. Let the filler dry for 24 hours. Apply a second coat if necessary.

FINISHES

Shellac is a hard finish that is easy to apply and dries in a few hours. For best results, thin the shellac slightly with alcohol and apply an extra coat or two. Several coats of thin shellac are much better than one or two thick coats. Sand the piece lightly with extra-fine sand paper between coats, then rub the entire surface with a dampened cloth.

Varnish is easy to brush on and dries to a smooth, hard finish within 24 hours. It makes an excellent finish that is transparent and gives a deep-finish look to your project. Be sure to apply varnish in a completely dust-free area. Apply one or two coats directly from the can with long even strokes. Rub between each coat. After the last coat, rub with 0000 steel wool.

Oil finishes are especially easy to use for the clock projects in this book. They are easy to apply, long lasting, never need sanding and actually improve the wood permanently. Apply a heavy, wet coat uniformly to all surfaces and let the finish dry for 20 or 30 minutes. Wipe the clock completely dry until you have a nice, satin finish.

PAINT

Five projects in this book require paint. The painted surface of these projects should look smooth with no hint of grain or a "wood look."

To achieve a smooth, painted finish, apply three or four coats of primer paint, sanding between each coat of paint. Apply at least two coats of paint. Sand between coats. After the last coat of paint, rub with #0000 steel wool. This will make the surface very smooth, but slightly dull. Apply a final coat of butcher wax to bring back the shine. This will give you a beautiful, satin-rich finish. Take care not to rub the paint off at the edges of the wood or molding.

CHAPTER 5

Making a Coffin Clock

Our goal in this demonstration is to show you the basic steps that go into making your own clock. We chose the coffin clock because it is a classic clock with simple lines. It also incorporates an "all-in-one" dial and bezel and a quartz movement. The complete plans for making the Shaker-Style Coffin Clock and a photograph of the finished clock are found on pages 138–140.

Plane the wood to the correct thickness. Each board will be planed to the thickness given in the parts list on page 139. Planing can also be done by hand.

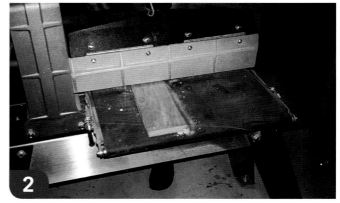

Sand the top and bottom surfaces.

Make a ¼" wide by ¼" deep rabbet in the two side pieces (part no. 1).

Locate and cut the 7½" diameter hole for the dial face in the front door (part no. 2).

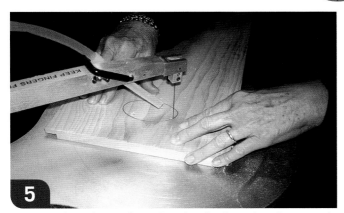

5 Locate and cut the 1¾" by 2¾" oval in the front door (part no. 2).

6 Make the two ⅝" wide by 5⁄16" deep rabbets in the door (part no. 2).

7 Sand the inside edges of the hole for the dial face and the pendulum hole.

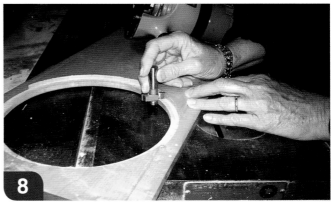

8 Using a router bit with a ball-bearing follower, make a rabbet ¼" deep and 5⁄16" wide to hold the glass in place.

9 Using a ¼" radius bit with a ball-bearing follower, give the two holes on the front door rounded edges.

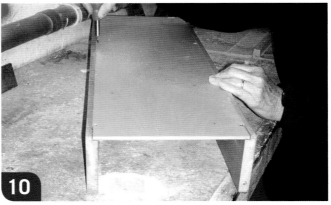

10 Glue and screw the back (part no. 3) to the two sides (part no. 1). Keep everything at 90 degrees.

11 Locate and add the two dial supports (part no. 7). Glue and screw in place.

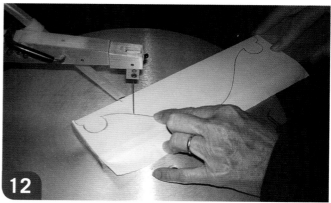

12 Layout and make the top splat (part no. 5). Sand all over.

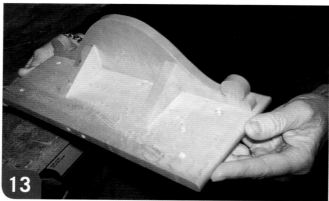

13 Glue up the top (part no. 4), the splat (part no. 5) and the two braces (part no. 6) as shown on the plans. The final assembly should look like this.

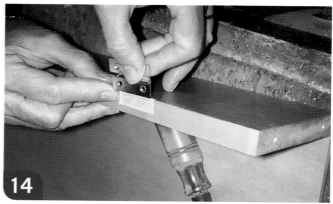

14 Locate and make two notches for the hinges on the right side of the clock case.

15 Attach the dial face to the backing board (part no. 8) with spray adhesive. Check to make sure it is the center of the opening.

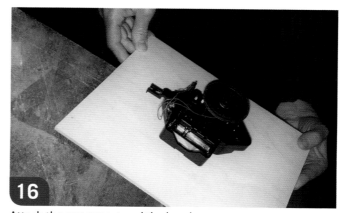

16 Attach the movement and the hands.

17 Screw the dial face and backing board in place so that the face appears in the center of the door hole cut out.

18 Attach the door. Check that it lines up correctly.

19 Attach the top and bottom (part no. 4) to the sides and back. Screw in place. Do not use any glue.

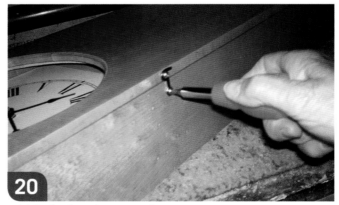

20 Add the latch and screw as shown.

21 Add the glass to the door (in the cut out sections) using black putty).

22 Add the long pendulum. You may have to add an extension to the rod so that the bob can be seen in the center of the little oval window.

Cat Lover's Wall Clock

Cats are always popular. If you like cats, this simple wall clock is just for you. Of course, it will also make a great gift for cat lovers. This sample was made of red elm. If you can find it, use ⅞-inch-thick wood.

SPECIAL INSTRUCTIONS

- Full-size pattern included in this book's envelope, or enlarge the pattern on p. 33.
- Choose an interesting piece of wood ¾" x 9¼" x 14¼".
- Add a hanger and a 2⁵⁄₁₆"-diameter insert.
- Insert 2⁵⁄₁₆"-dia.

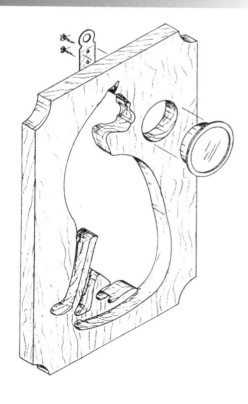

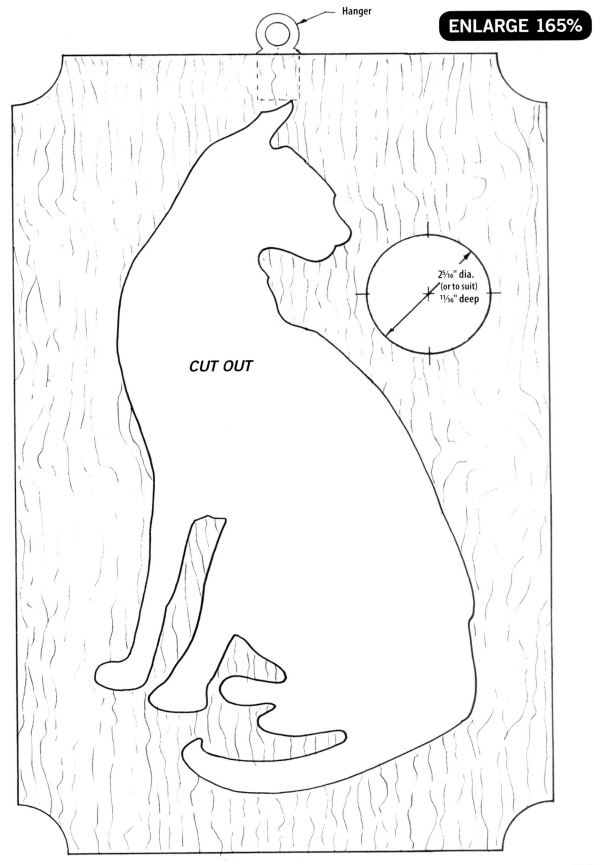

Hanger

ENLARGE 165%

2⁵⁄₁₆" dia.
(or to suit)
1¹⁄₁₆" deep

CUT OUT

Woodland Fawn Clock

This clock will make a great project for those in the family who love wildlife. It is a simple one-piece plaque-style clock. You might want to add a mirrored piece of Plexiglas behind the cut-out pattern to really enhance the clock.

SPECIAL INSTRUCTIONS

- Full-size pattern included in this book's envelope, or enlarge the pattern on p. 35.

- Choose a nice piece of wood ½" x 8½" x 9".

- Use a 1⅜" diameter Forstner bit to drill a ¼" deep hole for the movement.

- Add a 2" diameter insert.

- Add a Plexiglas® mirror (optional).

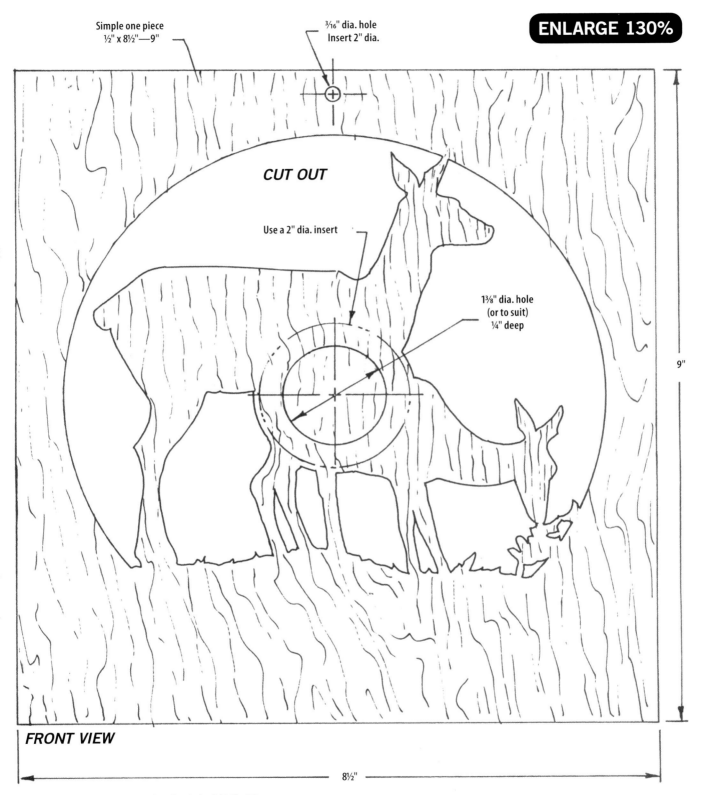

Simple one piece
½" x 8½"—9"

³⁄₁₆" dia. hole
Insert 2" dia.

ENLARGE 130%

CUT OUT

Use a 2" dia. insert

1³⁄₈" dia. hole
(or to suit)
¼" deep

9"

FRONT VIEW

8½"

Optional: Add mirror plexiglass in back (8½" x 9")

Super-Simple Desk Clock

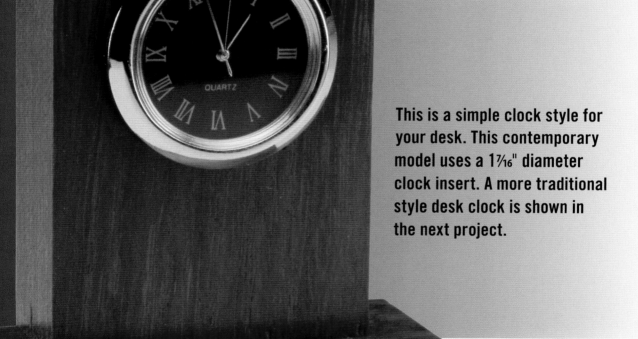

This is a simple clock style for your desk. This contemporary model uses a 1⁷⁄₁₆" diameter clock insert. A more traditional style desk clock is shown in the next project.

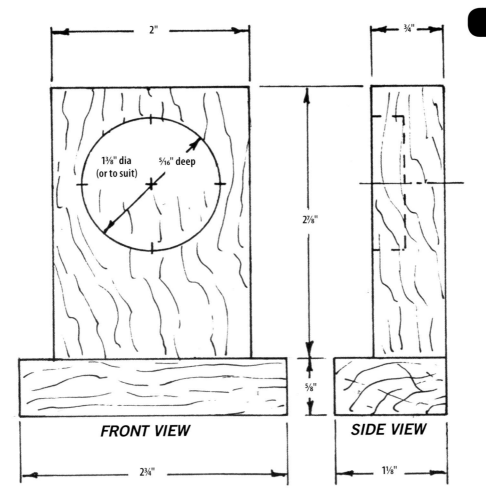

2"

¾"

1⅜" dia
(or to suit)

⁵⁄₁₆" deep

2⅞"

⅝"

FRONT VIEW

SIDE VIEW

2¾"

1⅛"

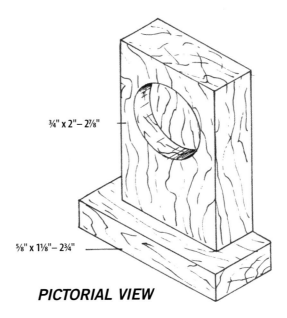

SPECIAL INSTRUCTIONS

- Use patterns at full size. Choose a nice hardwood and cut pieces to overall size. Locate and drill a 1⅜-inch-diameter hole, ⁵⁄₁₆ deep for the insert.

- Carefully glue the top section to the base as shown—take care not to let glue squeeze out over the base.

- Add four ½-inch-diameter felt pad feet (not shown).

- Use a 1⁷⁄₁₆" dia. mini insert.

¾" x 2" – 2⅞"

⅝" x 1⅛" – 2¾"

PICTORIAL VIEW

Angel Desk Clock

This is a simple clock style for your desk. It is very similar to the clock shown in the previous project. The rounded corners give this timepiece a more traditional look.

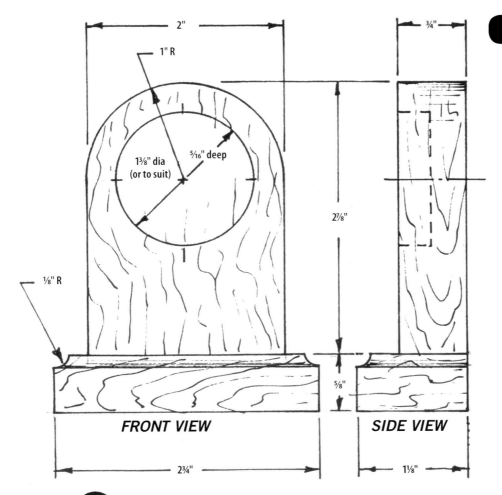

FRONT VIEW

SIDE VIEW

SPECIAL INSTRUCTIONS

- Use the patterns at full size. Choose a nice hardwood and cut pieces to overall size. Locate and drill a 1⅜-inch-diameter hole, 5/16" deep for the insert.

- Use a ⅛" radius router bit with a follower to make the cut for the base.

- Round the top section.

- Carefully glue the top section to the base as shown--- take care not to let glue squeeze out over the base.

- Add four ½-inch-diameter felt pad feet (not shown).

- Use a 1⁷⁄₁₆" dia. mini insert.

Business Clock

This project serves three functions: It holds business cards, tells the time and records the temperature. Be sure to make it out of a very special wood. Walnut, cherry or any unusual kind of wood is a good choice. This sample was made of cocobolo wood. You might want to use dollhouse hinges and catch if you can find them. Try using epoxy to anchor the hinges and latch in place rather than using short brass screws.

SPECIAL INSTRUCTIONS

- Use the patterns at full size.

- Choose special wood.

- Cut the wood to an overall size of 2¾" x 4½".

- In part No. 1, drill two 1⅜-inch-diameter by ⅜-inch-deep holes.

- In part No. 2, cut out the center section.

- Glue part No. 2 to part No. 3 and sand the edges.

- Attach two hinges, part No. 4.

- Sand all over.

- Attach clasp, part No. 5.

- Add lid stop, No. 9.

- Re-sand and stain to suit.

- Add the clock and a thermometer.

- Add felt pads to the bottom.

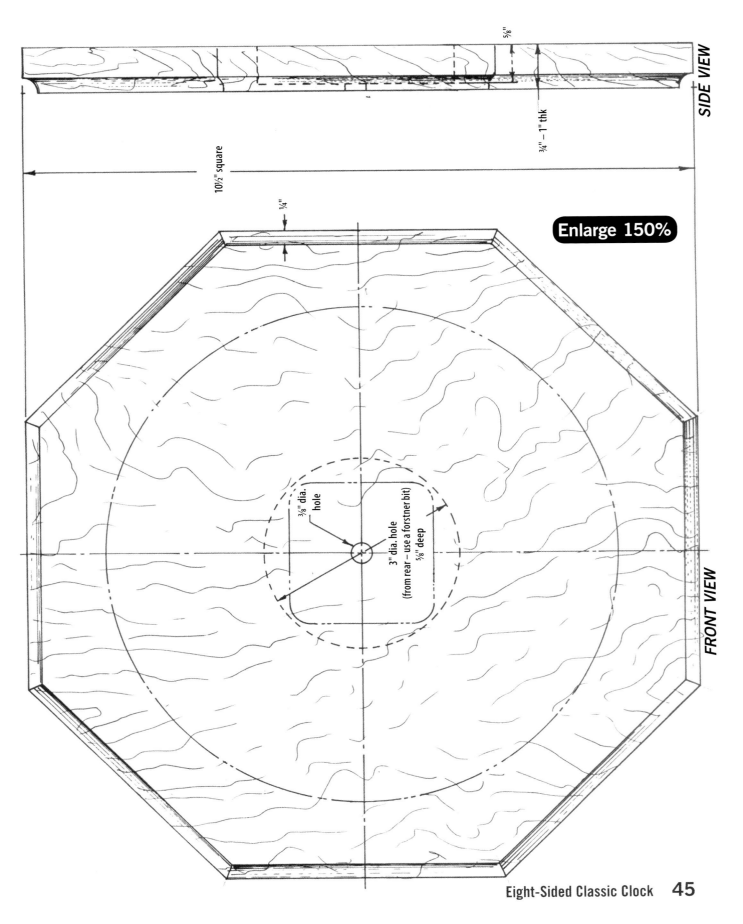

SIDE VIEW

5/8"

3/4" – 1" thk

10½" square

¼"

Enlarge 150%

3/8" dia. hole

3" dia. hole
(from rear – use a forstner bit)
5/8" deep

FRONT VIEW

Eight-Sided Classic Clock 45

Roman Corners Clock

If you need a wall clock for a modern setting, this clock is just right. It is a small, one-piece clock.

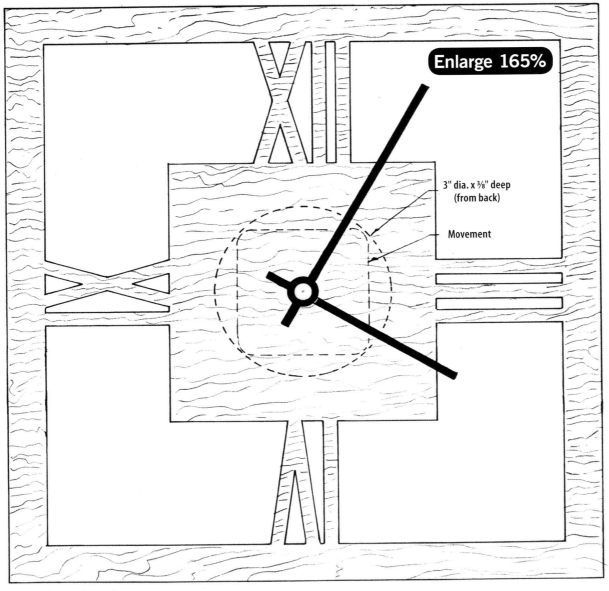

Enlarge 165%

3" dia. x ⅜" deep
(from back)

Movement

FRONT VIEW

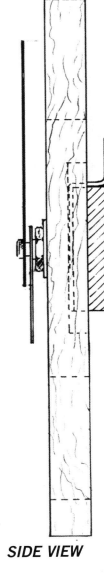

SIDE VIEW

SPECIAL INSTRUCTIONS

- Full-size patterns included in this book's envelope, or enlarge the patterns.

- Choose an interesting piece of hardwood.

- Locate the exact center and drill a ⁵⁄₁₆-inch-diameter hole from the front to the back.

- From the center of the ⁵⁄₁₆-inch-diameter hole and from the back of the piece, drill a 3-inch-diameter, ⅜-inch-deep hole with a Forstner bit.

- Make a copy of the face pattern, enlarging it to 165%. Glue to wood.

- Make all the interior cuts.

- Sand.

- Apply a clear coat top finish.

- Add the movement with the hanger attached.

- Add the hands and the battery.

- Material: ¾" x 10¼" – 10¼"

- 2⅛" square quartz movement

- Hands to suit

Trophy Buck Wall Clock

This is a wall clock for the deer hunter. It will surely be a hit for your den or playroom. The sample clock was made of avodire on walnut.

SPECIAL INSTRUCTIONS

- Full-size patterns included in this book's envelope, or enlarge the patterns on p. 49.

- Choose two kinds of wood: a light wood and a contrasting, darker wood. (Try using a light and dark stain if contrasting woods are not available.)

- Attach pattern to the ¼-inch-thick wood and cut it out.

- Cut a ¾-inch-thick backboard to 9½-inch-diameter.

- From the back, drill a 3½-inch-diameter, ½-inch-deep hole. With the 3½-inch-diameter hole as the center point, start at the back and drill a 5⁄16-inch-diameter hole through to the front.

- Sand all over. Stain to suit.

- Glue the front cut out to the backboard.

- Add the movement, hanger and hands (standard quartz movement with ¾" shaft length, hands to suit).

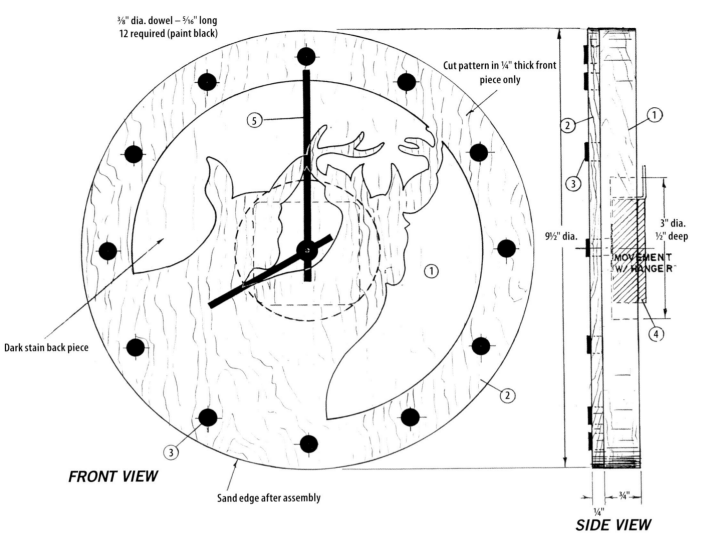

⅜" dia. dowel – ⁵⁄₁₆" long
12 required (paint black)

Cut pattern in ¼" thick front piece only

Dark stain back piece

FRONT VIEW

Sand edge after assembly

9½" dia.

3" dia.
½" deep

MOVEMENT
W/ HANGER

¼"   ¾"

SIDE VIEW

Enlarge 200%

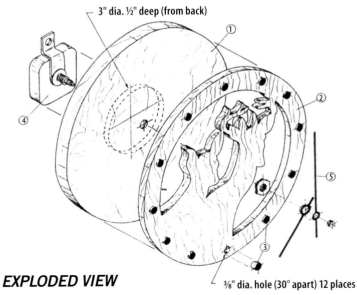

3" dia. ½" deep (from back)

EXPLODED VIEW

⅜" dia. hole (30° apart) 12 places

Writer's Desk Clock

This project adds class to any desk. It incorporates a clock, pen and pencil all wrapped up into one modern desk clock. The sample clock was made of walnut.

SPECIAL INSTRUCTIONS

- Choose an interesting hardwood. Cut it to size according to the cutting list.
- Follow the detail drawings to make all the pieces.
- In Part No. 2, drill a 2⅜-inch-diameter, ½-inch-deep hole using a Forstner.
- Sand all over. Stain to suit.
- Screw the post No. 2 to the base No. 1.
- Add the pen/pencil set.
- Add the insert and the felt pad feet.

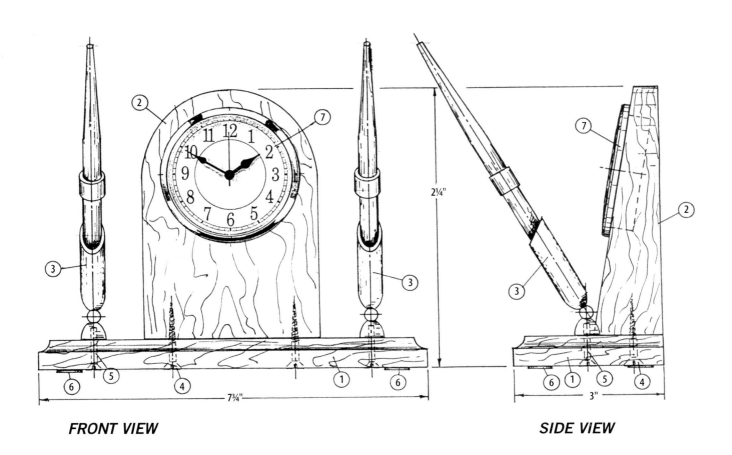

FRONT VIEW

SIDE VIEW

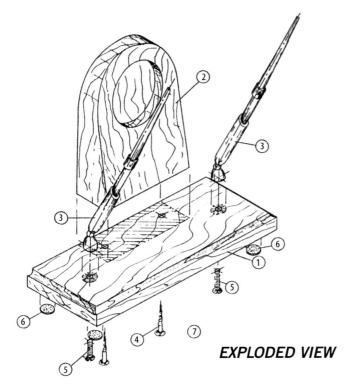

EXPLODED VIEW

No.	Name	Size	Qty
1	Base	⅝" x 3" – 7¾"	1
2	Post	1½" x 3½" – 5⅛"	1
3	Pen/pencil set	To suit	1
4	Flat head screw	#5 – 1¼" long	1 pr.
5	Flat head machine screw	To suit	1
6	Pad - felt	½" dia.	1
7	Insert	3" dia. or to suit	1

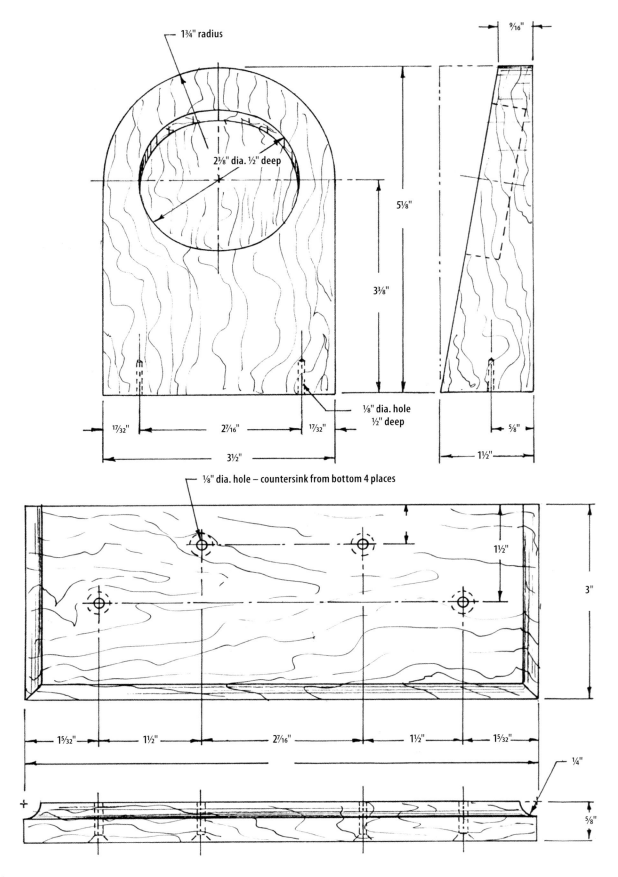

1¾" radius

2⅜" dia. ½" deep

9/16"

5⅛"

3⅜"

⅛" dia. hole
½" deep

17/32"

2⁷/16"

17/32"

3½"

5/8"

1½"

⅛" dia. hole – countersink from bottom 4 places

1½"

3"

1⁵/32"

1½"

2⁷/16"

1½"

1⁵/32"

¼"

5/8"

Pyramid Desk Clock

This is a simple but interesting desk clock. It looks good with a natural finish or painted. The model clock was made of zebra wood on purpleheart with pau amarello in the center.

SPECIAL INSTRUCTIONS

- Cut the triangle from a 1¾-inch-thick piece of wood. (If you can't find wood that inch thick, glue up two ¾-inch-thick pieces sandwiched between one ¼-inch-thick piece.

- Cut the triangle to size and sand all over.

- Make a ⅛-inch radius contour around the front (optional) using a router bit with a follower.

- From the back, drill a 3⅜-inch-diameter 1-inch-deep hole with a Forstner bit.

- Sand all over. Stain or paint to suit.

- Add felt pads.

- Add a movement with batteries.

- Add the hands.

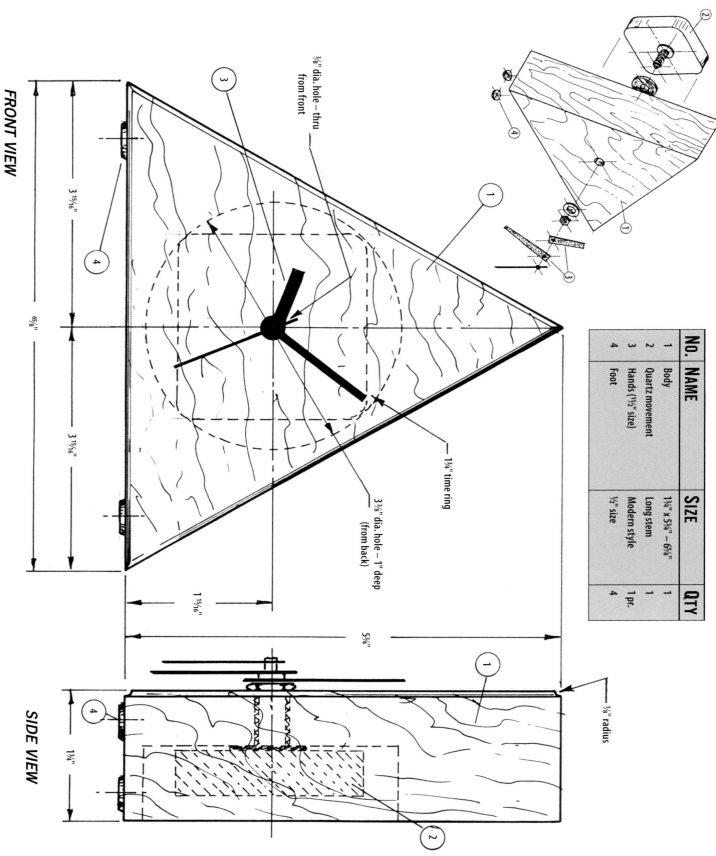

FRONT VIEW

SIDE VIEW

3/8" dia. hole – thru
from front

3 15/16"

6 5/8"

3 15/16"

1 3/4" time ring

3 3/8" dia. hole – 1" deep
(from back)

1 15/16"

5 3/4"

1/8" radius

1 3/4"

NO.	NAME	SIZE	QTY
1	Body	1 3/4" x 5 3/4" — 6 5/8"	1
2	Quartz movement	Long stem	1
3	Hands (1 1/2" size)	Modern style	1
4	Foot	1/2" size	4

Sextant Desk Clock

Here is an unusual desk or shelf clock. It should be made of a nice hardwood. This model clock was made of goncolo alves wood.

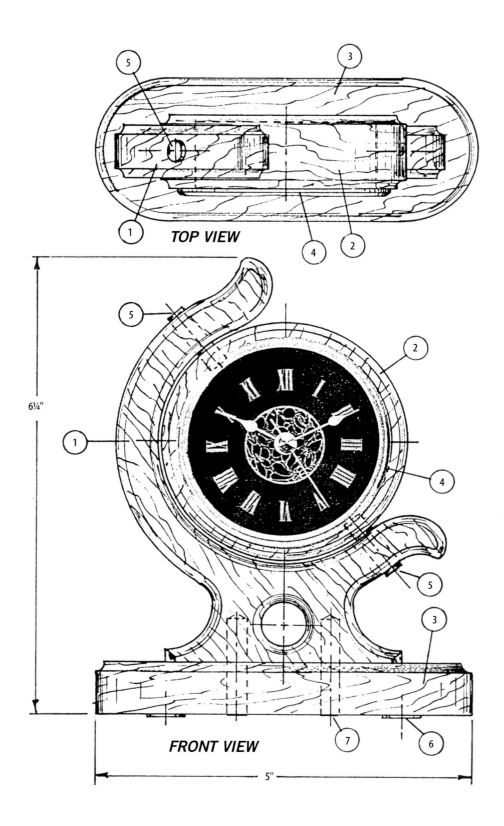

TOP VIEW

FRONT VIEW

6¼"

5"

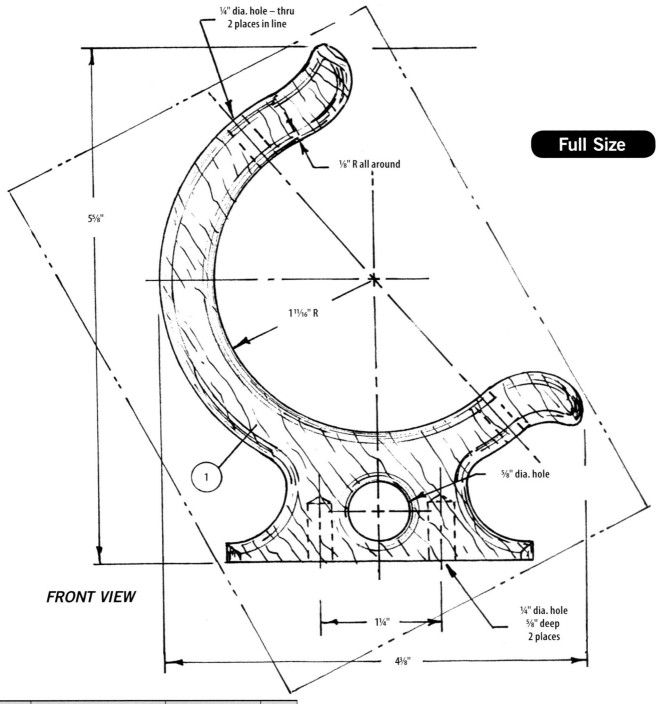

¼" dia. hole – thru
2 places in line

⅛" R all around

Full Size

5⅝"

1¹¹⁄₁₆" R

①

⅝" dia. hole

FRONT VIEW

1¼"

4⅜"

¼" dia. hole
⅝" deep
2 places

No.	Name	Size	Qty
1	Support	¾" x 4¼" – 6⅛"	1
2	Doughnut	1 x 3½" – 3½"	1
3	Base	¾" x 2" – 5"	1
4	Insert	2¹³⁄₁₆" dia.	1
5	Peg	¼" dia. – 1" lg.	2
6	Foot - felt	½" dia.	4
7	Pin	¼" dia. – 1¼" lg.	2

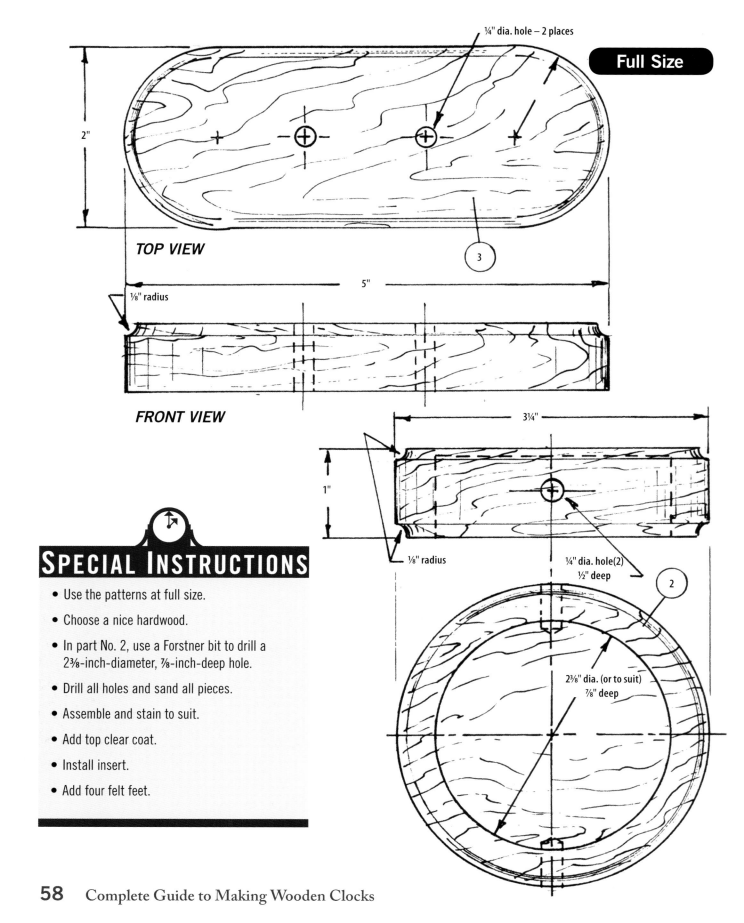

¼" dia. hole – 2 places

Full Size

2"

TOP VIEW

3

⅛" radius

5"

FRONT VIEW

⅛" radius

3¼"

1"

¼" dia. hole(2)
½" deep

2

2⅜" dia. (or to suit)
⅞" deep

SPECIAL INSTRUCTIONS

- Use the patterns at full size.
- Choose a nice hardwood.
- In part No. 2, use a Forstner bit to drill a 2⅜-inch-diameter, ⅞-inch-deep hole.
- Drill all holes and sand all pieces.
- Assemble and stain to suit.
- Add top clear coat.
- Install insert.
- Add four felt feet.

Balloon Shelf Clock

This clock design is taken from an original antique clock. It is an interesting design and will add a little formality to any room. The model clock was made of purpleheart wood.

SPECIAL INSTRUCTIONS

- Glue four ½-inch-thick pieces of wood together for the 2-inch-thick body. (4" x 6¼")

- Use a photocopier to enlarge the pattern 125%.

- Drill a 2⅜-diameter hole, ⅞-inches-deep for the insert.

- Make the base as shown and attach the body assembly.

- Sand all over and stain to suit.

- Apply a clear top coat.

- Add four ¾-inch-diameter feet.

- Add the insert with batteries.

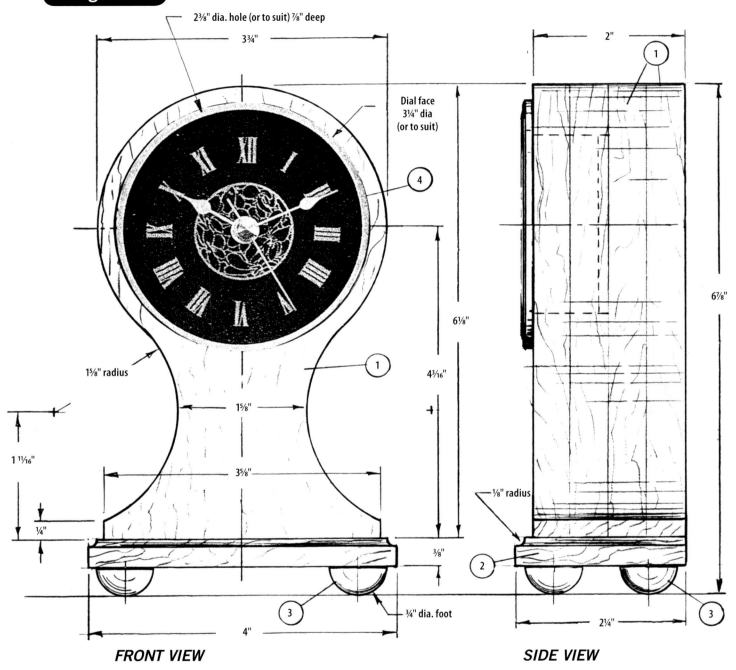

Enlarge 125%

2⅜" dia. hole (or to suit) ⅞" deep

3¾"

Dial face
3¼" dia
(or to suit)

④

2"

①

1⅝" radius

①

6⅛"

4³⁄₁₆"

6⅞"

1⅝"

3⅝"

1 ¹¹⁄₁₆"

⅛" radius

¼"

②

⅜"

③

¾" dia. foot

4"

2¼"

③

FRONT VIEW

SIDE VIEW

No.	Name	Size	Qty
1	Body	½" x 4" – 6¼"	4
2	Base	⅜" x 2¼" – 4"	1
3	Foot	¾" dia.	4
4	Insert	¾" dia.	1

In-the-Balance Shelf Clock

This clock is truly modern and will really make the setting for modern décor. It is unusual. Pau almarello and morado wood was used in making this clock.

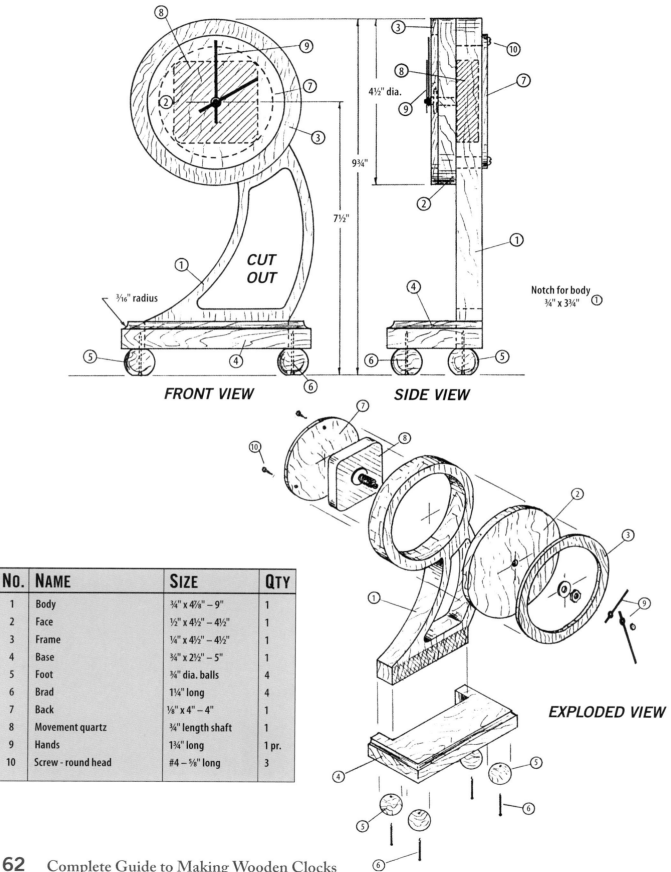

CUT OUT

FRONT VIEW

SIDE VIEW

EXPLODED VIEW

³⁄₁₆" radius

4½" dia.

9¾"

7½"

Notch for body
¾" x 3¾"

No.	Name	Size	Qty
1	Body	¾" x 4⅞" – 9"	1
2	Face	½" x 4½" – 4½"	1
3	Frame	¼" x 4½" – 4½"	1
4	Base	¾" x 2½" – 5"	1
5	Foot	¾" dia. balls	4
6	Brad	1¼" long	4
7	Back	⅛" x 4" – 4"	1
8	Movement quartz	¾" length shaft	1
9	Hands	1¾" long	1 pr.
10	Screw - round head	#4 – ⅝" long	3

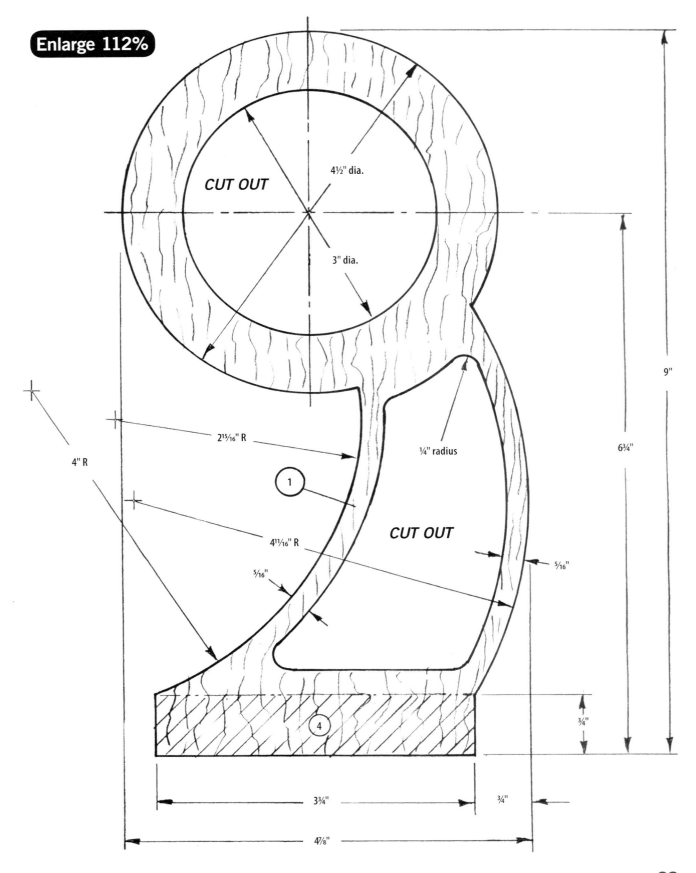

Enlarge 112%

CUT OUT

4½" dia.

3" dia.

2¹⁵⁄₁₆" R

¼" radius

4" R

1

CUT OUT

4¹¹⁄₁₆" R

⁵⁄₁₆"

⁵⁄₁₆"

4

9"

6¾"

¾"

3¾"

¾"

4⅞"

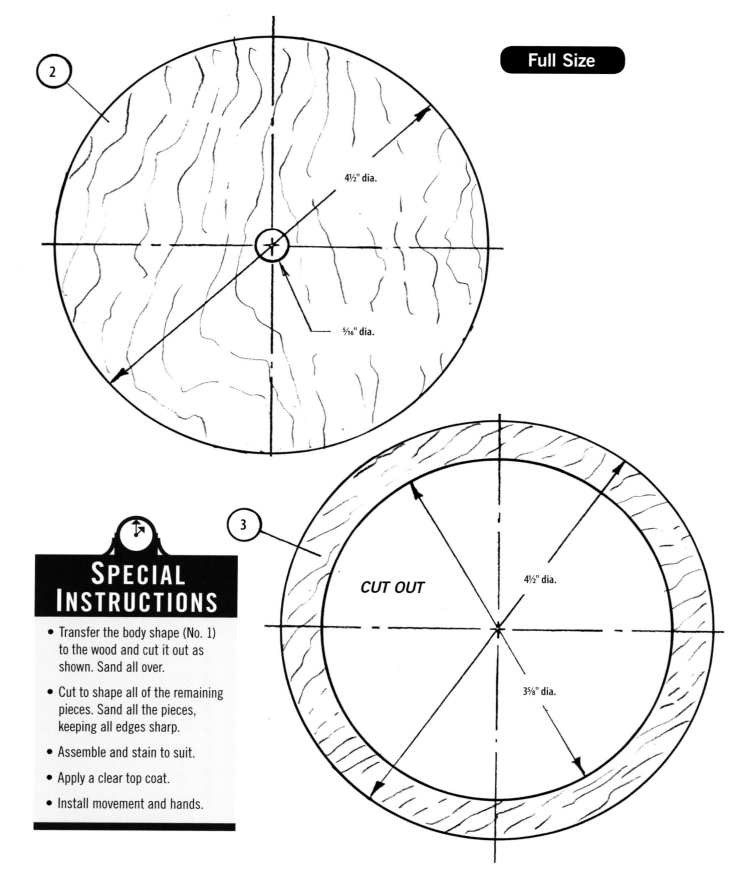

Full Size

2   4½" dia.

5⁄16" dia.

SPECIAL INSTRUCTIONS

- Transfer the body shape (No. 1) to the wood and cut it out as shown. Sand all over.

- Cut to shape all of the remaining pieces. Sand all the pieces, keeping all edges sharp.

- Assemble and stain to suit.

- Apply a clear top coat.

- Install movement and hands.

3

CUT OUT

4½" dia.

3⅝" dia.

Tambour Shelf Clock

Tambour clocks are still in fashion, as they were in 1910. They were one of the most enduring clock designs ever made. Walnut with satinwood accents were used in this clock.

SPECIAL INSTRUCTIONS

- Use full-size patterns in this book's envelope, or enlarge patterns on pages 75–76.

- Cut out pieces No. 1 and 2 with a band saw and than sand all over.

- Locate and drill a ⅞ inch deep, 3⅛-inch-diameter hole.

- Cut part No. 6 out of a piece of a very unusual piece of ⅛" x 1" - 5⅞" piece of wood. Stain or paint yellow (optional).

- Assemble the body with the base and stain to suit.

- Locate and glue in place the trim (part No. 6).

- Apply two coats of clear top coat.

- Add the feet and insert.

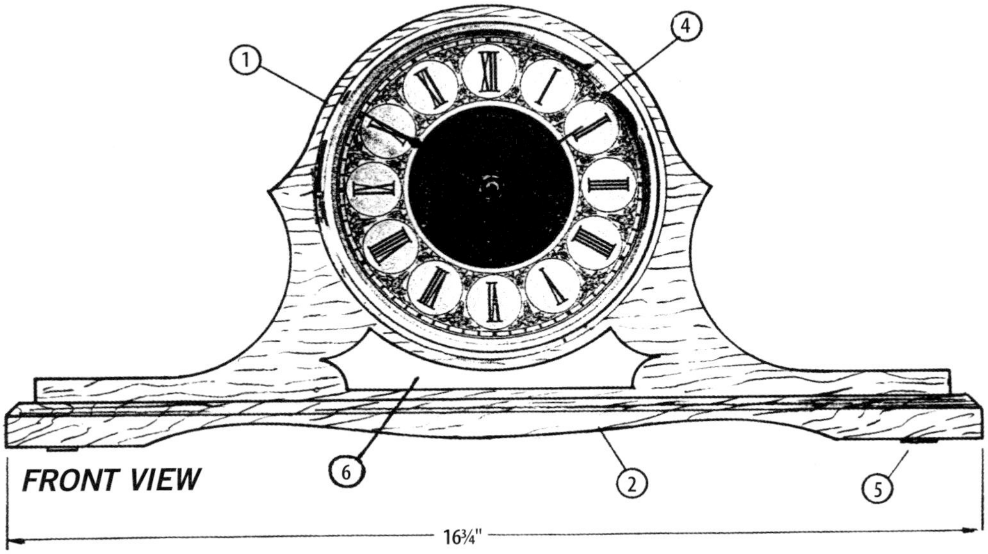

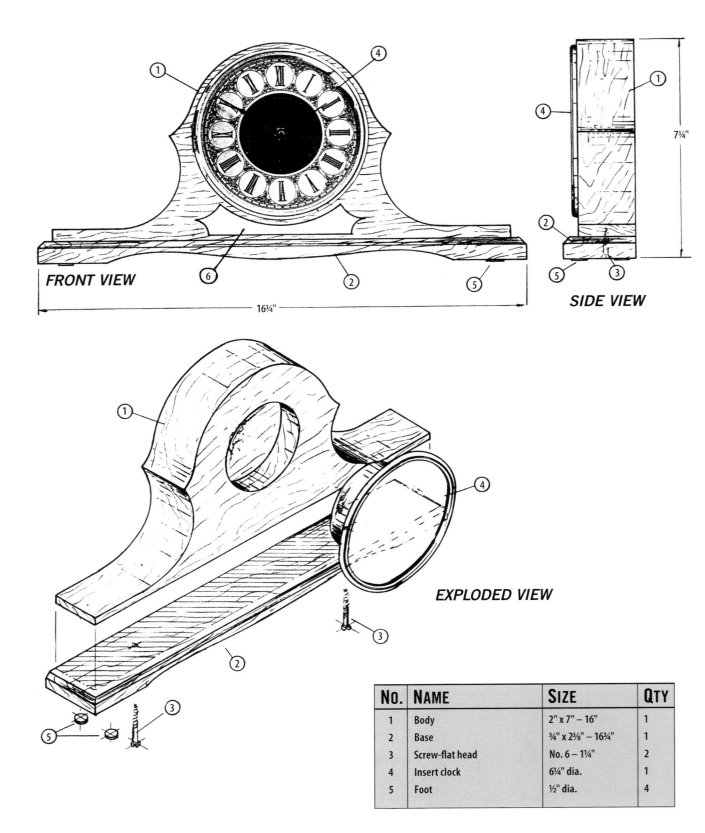

FRONT VIEW

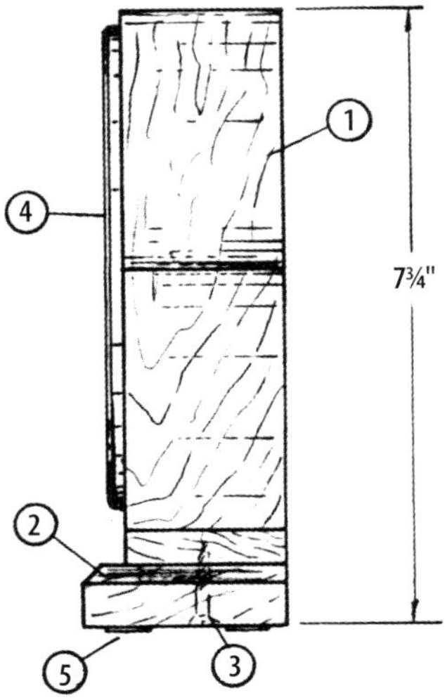

SIDE VIEW

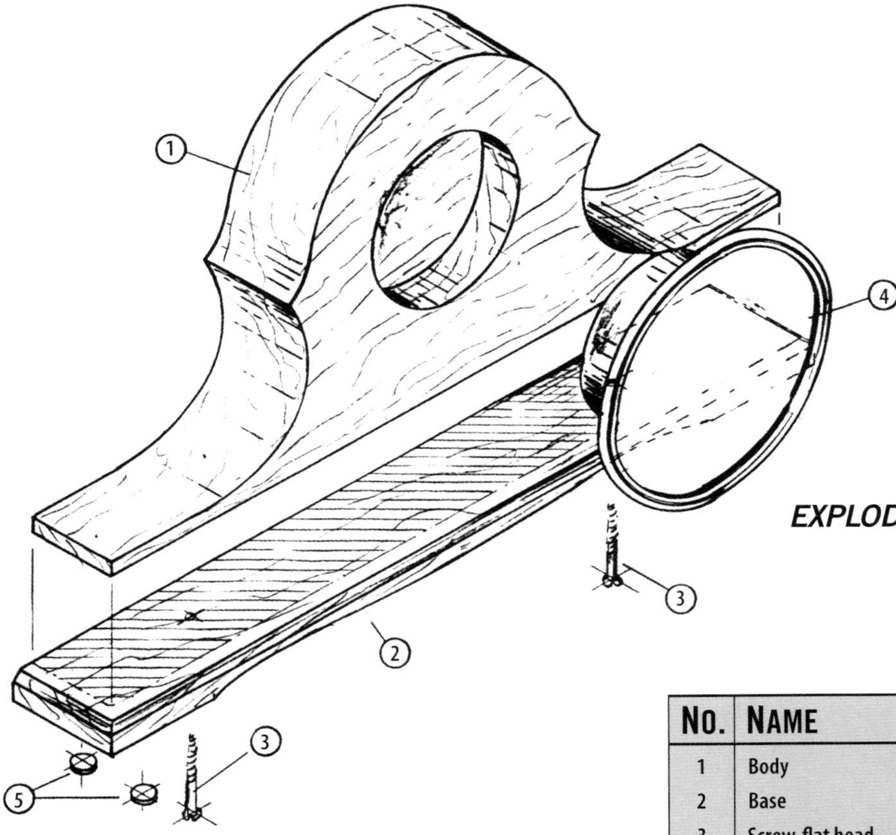

EXPLODED VIEW

No.	Name	Size	Qty
1	Body	2" x 7" – 16"	1
2	Base	¾" x 2⅜" – 16¾"	1
3	Screw-flat head	No. 6 – 1¼"	2
4	Insert clock	6¼" dia.	1
5	Foot	½" dia.	4

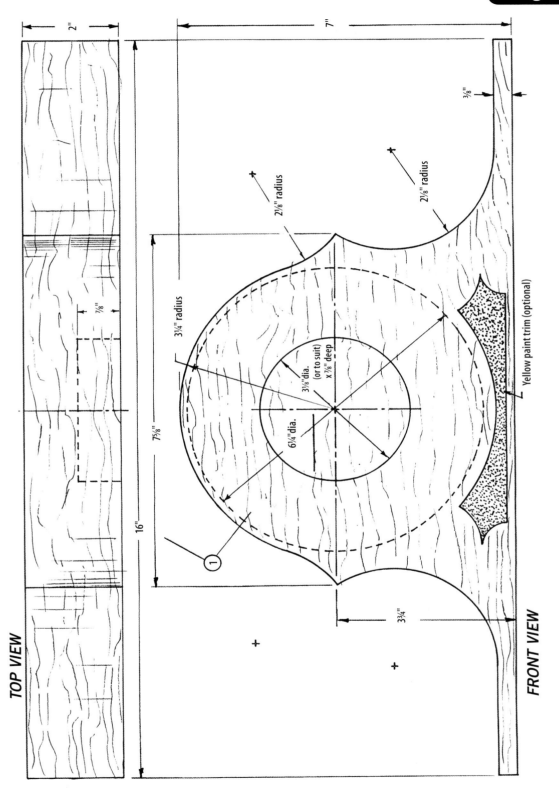

TOP VIEW

2"

7⁄8"

16"

7"

3⁄8"

2⅛" radius

2⅛" radius

3¼" radius

7⅞"

3⅛" dia.
(or to suit)
x 7⁄8" deep

6¼" dia.

①

3¾"

Yellow paint trim (optional)

FRONT VIEW

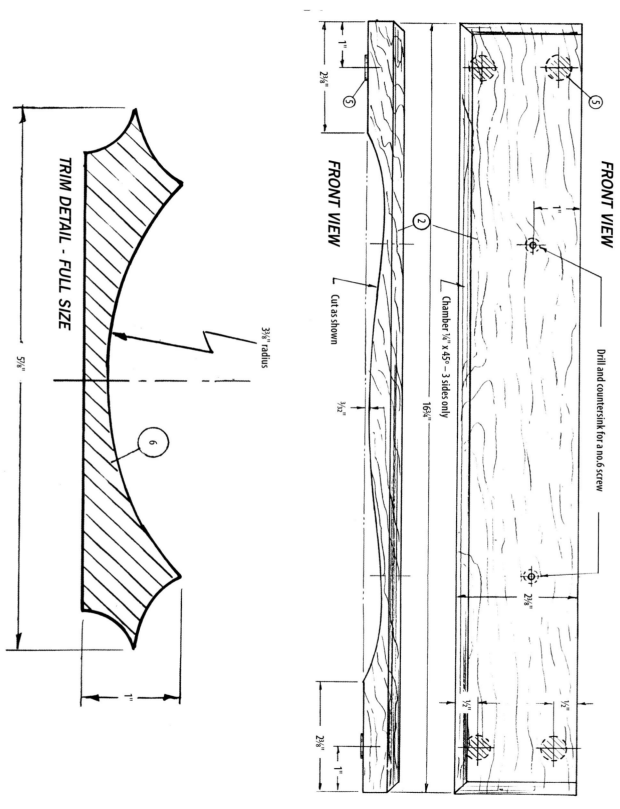

TRIM DETAIL - FULL SIZE

5⅞"

3⅜" radius

1"

6

FRONT VIEW

1"

2⅜"

5

Cut as shown

3/32"

Chamber ¼" x 45º – 3 sides only

16¾"

2

FRONT VIEW

5

Drill and countersink for a no.6 screw

1"

2⅜"

1"

2⅜"

½"

½"

Petite Shelf Clock

This pretty little clock will add warmth to any room. Reminiscent of the Victorian age, it is a great clock for a young girl's room. This sample was made of white oak with a purpleheart accent. The design is based on an original antique clock.

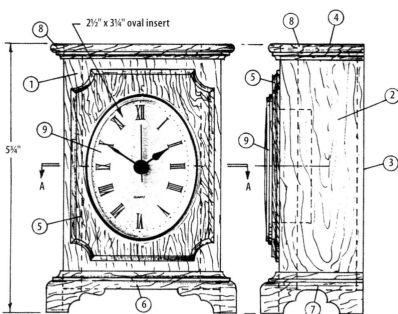

FRONT VIEW   **SIDE VIEW**

ASSEMBLY VIEW

2½" x 3¼" oval insert

5¾"

No.	Name	Size	Qty
1	Front	³⁄₈" x 3⁵⁄₁₆" – 5"	1
2	Side	³⁄₈" x 1¹¹⁄₁₆" – 5"	2
3	Back	⅛" x 3¹⁄₁₆" – 5"	1
4	Top	⅛" x 3¹³⁄₁₆" – 3⁵⁄₁₆"	1
5	Trim - Middle	³⁄₁₆" x 3 – 4"	1
6	Molding - Front	³⁄₈" x ⅞" – 4¹⁄₁₆"	
7	Molding - Side	³⁄₈" x ⅞" – 2³⁄₁₆"	
8	Molding - Top (cut to fit)	⁵⁄₁₆" x ⁹⁄₁₆" – 12"	
9	Oval Insert	2½" x 3¼"	

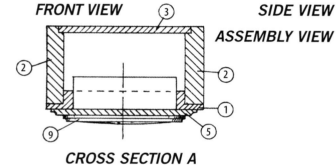

CROSS SECTION A

SPECIAL INSTRUCTIONS

- Use a contrasting wood for part No. 5.

- Make the molding as shown or as close as possible using whatever router bits you have.

- Dry fit all the pieces and adjust if necessary.

- Glue all pieces together.

- Sand all over and apply one or two clear top coats.

- Add the insert.

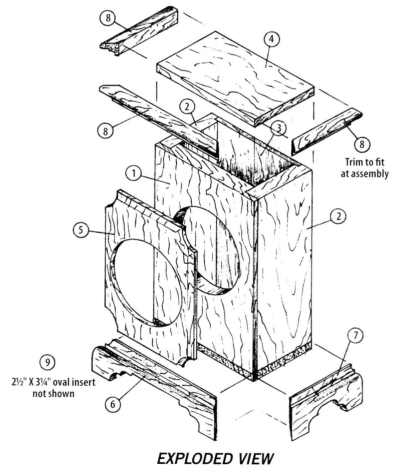

Trim to fit at assembly

2½" X 3¼" oval insert not shown

EXPLODED VIEW

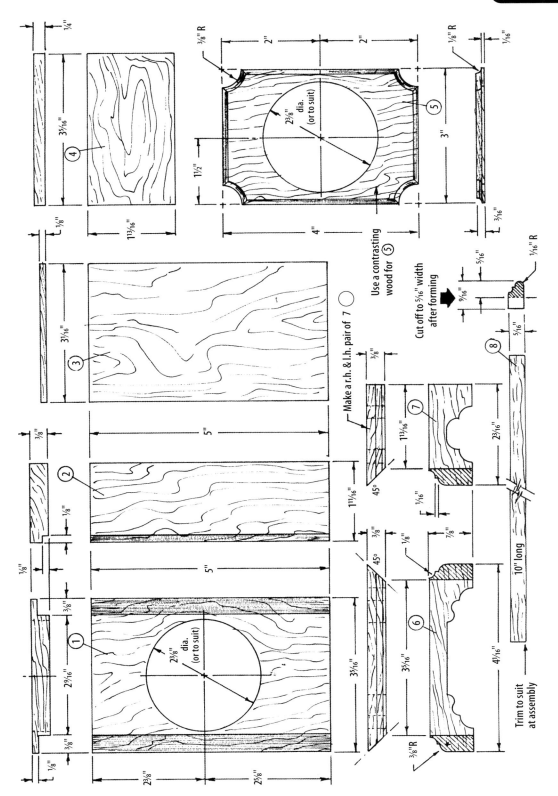

¼"

3⁵⁄₁₆"

④

1¹³⁄₁₆"

⅛"

3¹⁄₁₆"

③

3⁄₈"

⅛"

②

5"

1⅛"

⅛"

3⁄₈"

⅛"

①

2⁹⁄₁₆"

3⁄₈"

⅛"

2⅜"

2⅝"

5"

3⁵⁄₁₆"

2³⁄₈" dia.
(or to suit)

3⁄₈" R

2"   2"

⅛" R   ¹⁄₁₆"

⑤

1½"

3"

3⁄₁₆"

4"

Use a contrasting wood for ⑤

Make a r.h. & l.h. pair of ⑦

3⁄₈"

45°

1¹³⁄₁₆"

⑦

⅛"

¹⁄₁₆"

3⁄₈"

45°

⅛"

⑥

3⁵⁄₁₆"

7⁄₈"

3⁄₈" R

Cut off to ⁵⁄₁₆" width after forming

¹⁄₁₆" R

5⁄₁₆"

9⁄₁₆"

5⁄₁₆"

⑧

2³⁄₁₆"

10" long

4¹⁄₁₆"

Trim to suit at assembly

19th-Century Shelf Clock

If you like antique projects, you will really like this pretty, original shelf clock.

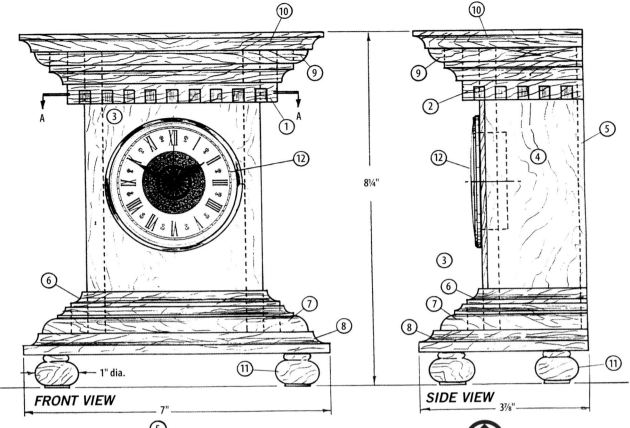

FRONT VIEW

1" dia.

8¼"

7"

SIDE VIEW

3⅞"

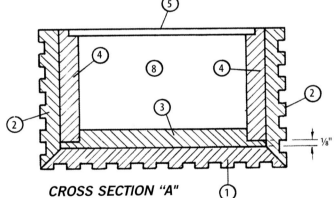

CROSS SECTION "A"

⅛"

NO.	NAME	SIZE	QTY
1	Front dentil	⅜" x 1¼" – 4¾" long	1
2	Side dentil	⅜" x 1¼" – 2¾" long	2
3	Face	⅜" x 4" – 6⅝" long	1
4	Side	⅜" x 2¼" – 6⅝" long	2
5	Back (pine)	⅛" x 3⅝" – 6⅝" long	1
6	Trim bottom	⅜" x 1" – 12" long	1
7	Trim bottom	⅝" x ⅝" – 16" long	1
8	Base	½" x 3⅞" – 7" long	1
9	Trim top	¾" x ¾" – 18" long	1
10	Top	⅜" x 3⅞" – 7" long	1
11	Foot	1" dia. x 1⅛" long	4
12	Insert		1

SPECIAL INSTRUCTIONS

- Use a photocopier to enlarge the pattern 165%.

- Study the exploded view so you will know how it all goes together.

- Cut all the pieces to overall size and sand the front and back surfaces.

- Make all parts per the detailed drawings and the exploded view.

- The 4 feet (part No. 11) can be turned or purchased. One-inch-diameter ball feet could be substituted if necessary.

- Dry fit all pieces.

- Sand all pieces.

- If everything fits correctly, assemble the pieces.

- Apply a stain (optional) and three clear top coats.

- Install the insert.

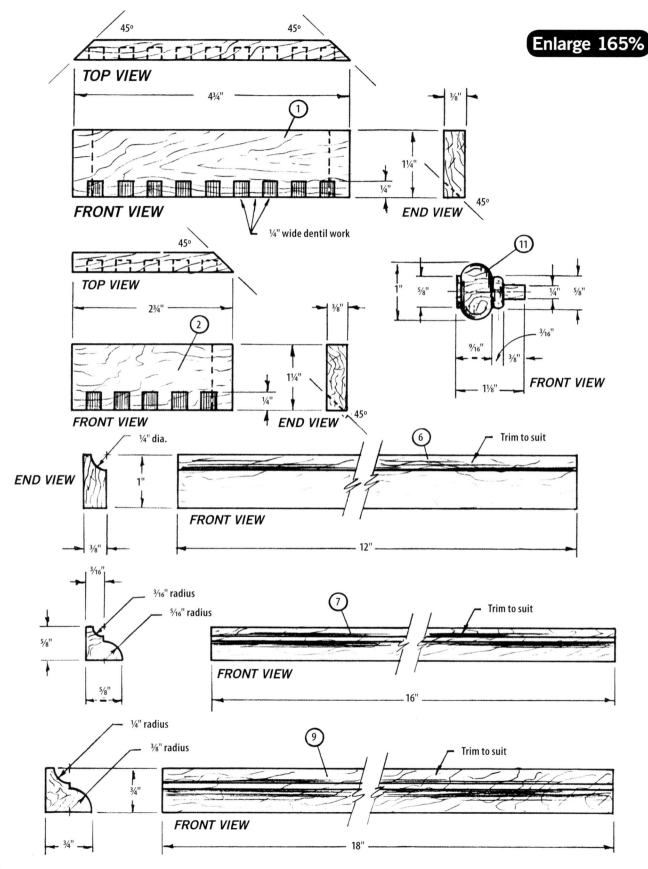

45°   45°

TOP VIEW

4¾"

3/8"

1

1¼"

¼"

FRONT VIEW

END VIEW   45°

¼" wide dentil work

45°

TOP VIEW

2¾"

3/8"

2

1¼"

¼"

FRONT VIEW

END VIEW   45°

11

1"   5/8"   ¼"   5/8"

9/16"   3/8"   3/16"

1⅛"

FRONT VIEW

¼" dia.

END VIEW

1"

3/8"

6   Trim to suit

FRONT VIEW

12"

3/16"

3/16" radius

5/16" radius

5/8"

5/8"

7   Trim to suit

FRONT VIEW

16"

¼" radius

3/8" radius

¾"

9   Trim to suit

FRONT VIEW

¾"

18"

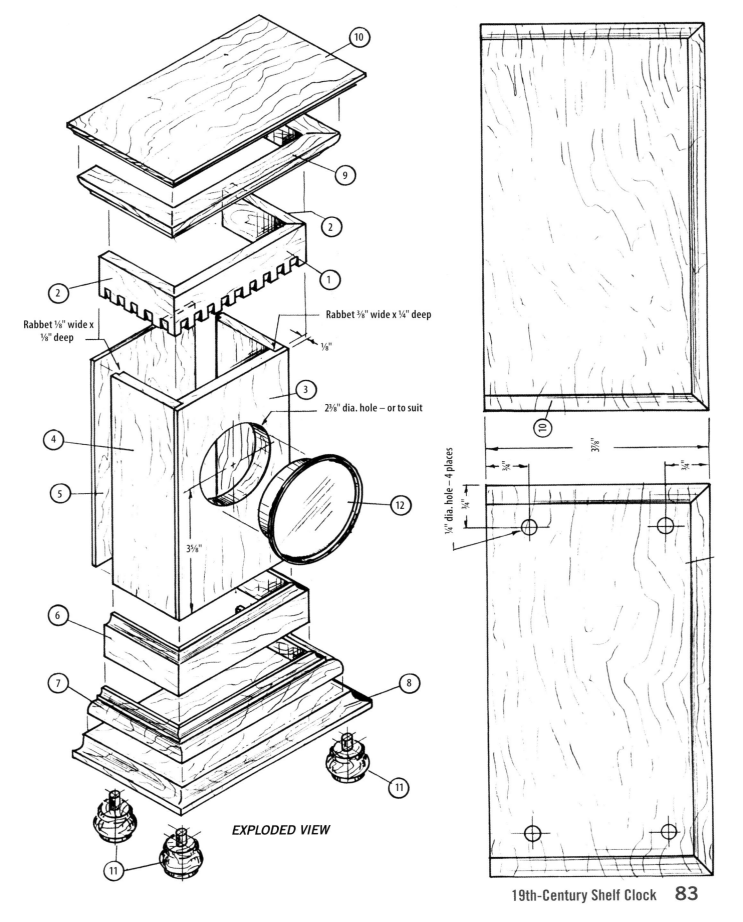

Rabbet ⅛" wide x ⅛" deep

Rabbet ⅜" wide x ¼" deep

⅛"

2⅜" dia. hole – or to suit

3⅝"

¼" dia. hole – 4 places

¾"

¾"

3⅞"

¾"

¾"

EXPLODED VIEW

19th-Century Shelf Clock 83

Lion's Head Black Mantel Clock

This clock is an exact copy of an original antique black mantel clock. You still can get copies of the original lion heads, feet and trim. Originals actually had wonderful movements. A good wood choice would be yellow poplar painted with black lacquer.

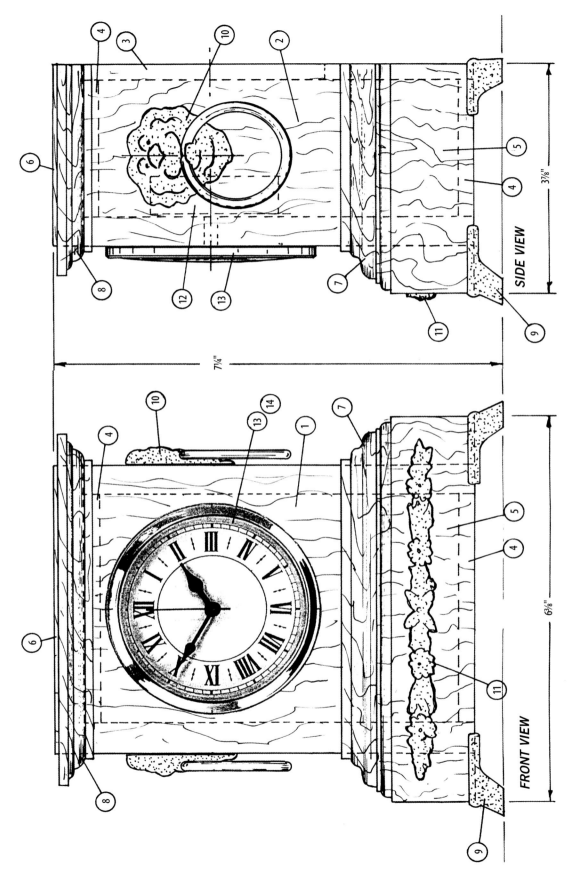

SIDE VIEW

FRONT VIEW

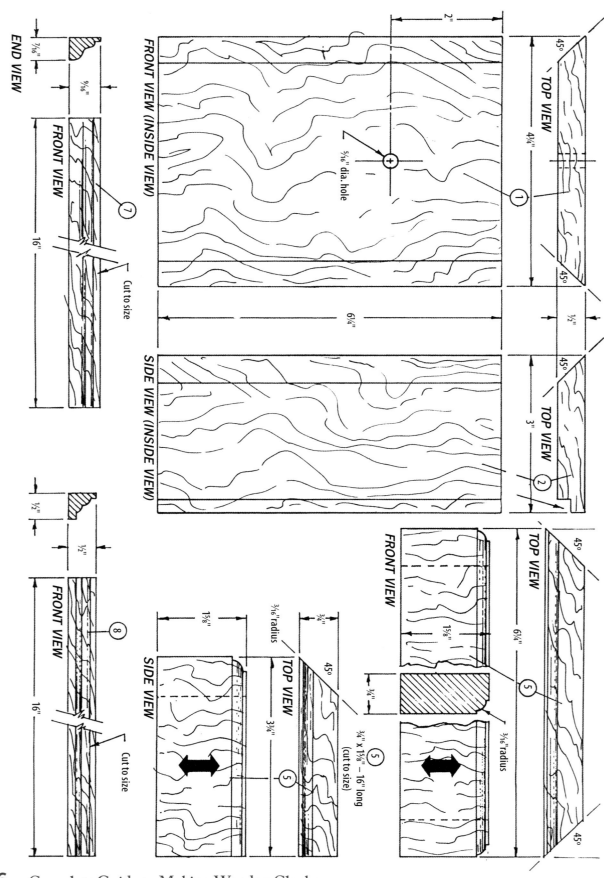

END VIEW

FRONT VIEW

⑦

Cut to size

16"

7/16"

9/16"

FRONT VIEW (INSIDE VIEW)

2"

TOP VIEW

4¾"

5/16" dia. hole

①

45°

45°

SIDE VIEW (INSIDE VIEW)

6¼"

½"

45°

TOP VIEW

3"

②

FRONT VIEW

⑧

Cut to size

16"

½"

½"

FRONT VIEW

TOP VIEW

45°

6¼"

1⅝"

¾"

⑤

3/16" radius

¾"

3/16" radius

¾" x 1⅝" — 16" long
(cut to size)

⑤

SIDE VIEW

1⅝"

3/16" radius

¾"

TOP VIEW

3¾"

45°

⑤

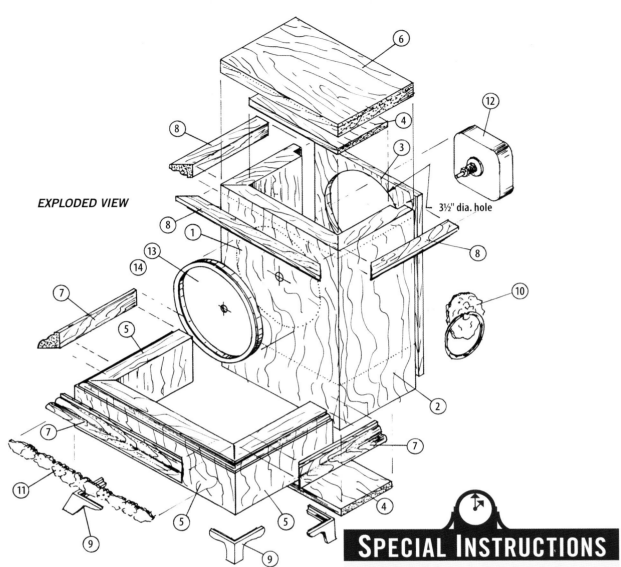

EXPLODED VIEW

3½" dia. hole

No.	Name	Size	Qty
1	Front	½" x 4¾"–6¼"	1
2	Side	½" x 3"–6¼"	2
3	Back (pine)	¼" x 3¾"–6¼"	1
4	Top/bottom (pine)	¼" x 2¼"–3¾"	2
5	Base (cut to size)	¾" x 1⅝"–16"	1
6	Top	½" x 3"–4¾"	1
7	Bottom molding	⁷⁄₁₆" x ⁹⁄₁₆"–16"	1
8	Top molding	½" x ½"–16"	1
9	Foot	as shown	1 set
10	Lion Head	as shown	2
11	Ornament	as shown	1
12	Movement quartz	as shown	1
13	Dial/bezel	3¼" to 3½" dia.	1
14	Hands	to suit	1 pair

SPECIAL INSTRUCTIONS

- Make moldings as close as possible to the design illustrated.

- Dry fit all the pieces as you go.

- Sand all the pieces, taking care to keep sharp edges.

- Assemble and glue the pieces together.

- Apply 3 or 4 coats of primer, sanding between each coat. Original black mantel clocks had a beautiful glass-like finish.

- Apply two coats of high gloss, black lacquer.

- Add the feet, trim and dial/bezel.

- Add the movement with hands.

- Apply a coat of butcher wax.

Kitchen Clock with Drawer

This clock makes a great kitchen clock. It can be stained or painted to match the room. The drawer gives you a little added storage space. A nice wood choice would be butternut because of its unusual character.

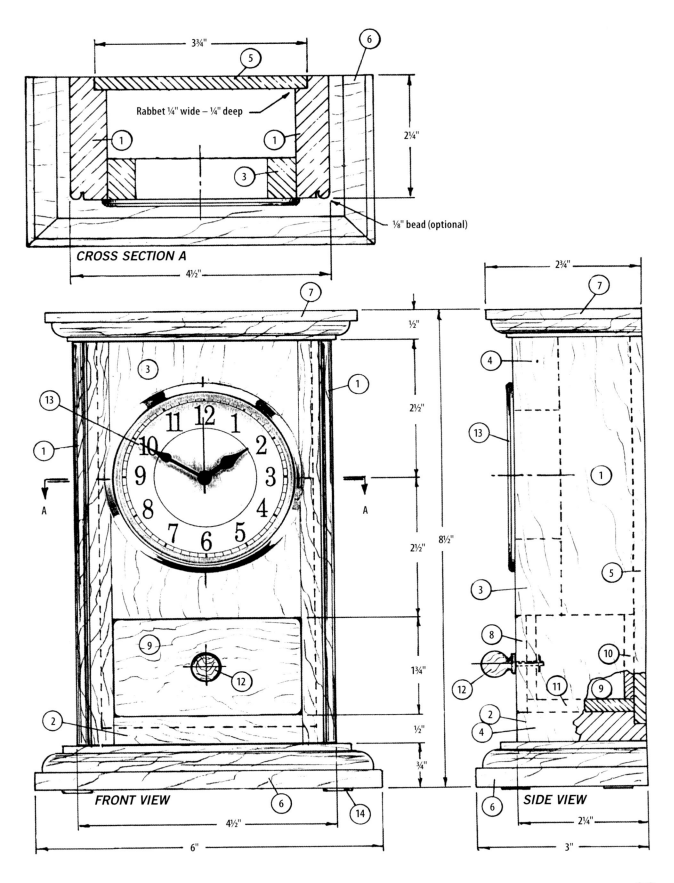

CROSS SECTION A

3¾"

5

6

Rabbet ¼" wide — ¼" deep

1

1

3

2¼"

⅛" bead (optional)

4½"

7

3

1

13

1

A

A

12 1 2 3 4 5 6 7 8 9 10 11

9

12

2

FRONT VIEW

6

14

½"

2½"

2½"

1¾"

½"

¾"

8½"

4½"

6"

2¾"

7

4

13

1

5

3

8

12

11

10

9

2

4

6

SIDE VIEW

2¼"

3"

Kitchen Clock with Drawer 89

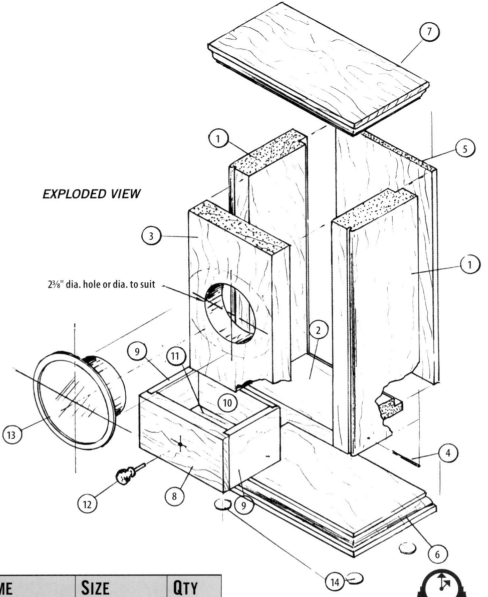

EXPLODED VIEW

2⅜" dia. hole or dia. to suit

No.	Name	Size	Qty
1	Side	¾" x 2¼" – 7¼"	2
2	Sub-base	½" x 2¼" – 3¼"	1
3	Front	¾" x 3¼" – 5"	1
4	Brad	¾" long	as req'd
5	Back	¼" x 3¾" – 7"	1
6	Base	¾" x 3" – 6"	1
7	Top	½" x 2¾" – 5½"	1
8	Drawer - front	⅜" x 1¾" – 3¼"	1
9	Drawer - side	¼" x 1¾" – 2"	2
10	Drawer - back	¼" x 1¾" – 3"	1
11	Drawer - bottom	¼" x 1⅝" – 2¾"	1
12	Drawer- pull	½" dia.	1
13	Movement - quartz	3¼" dia.	1
14	Foot - felt	½" dia.	4

SPECIAL INSTRUCTIONS

- Cut and fit all pieces per the exploded view and assembly views.

- Dry fit all pieces.

- If the fit is correct, glue the pieces together.

- Fit the drawer to the opening.

- Sand all over.

- Stain or paint to suit.

- Add the feet and insert.

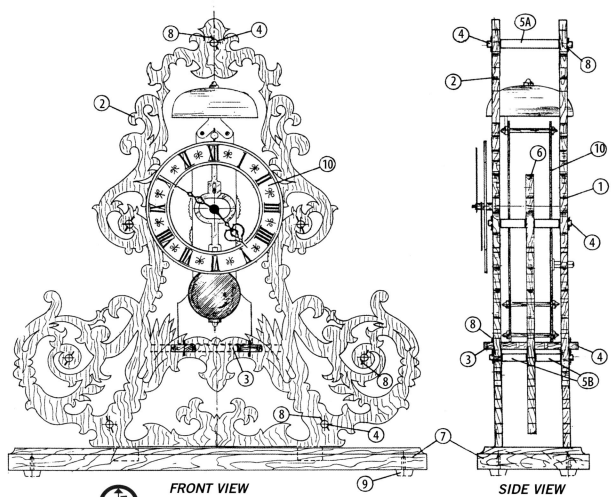

FRONT VIEW

SIDE VIEW

ASSEMBLY

SPECIAL INSTRUCTIONS

- Use full-size patterns included in this book's envelope, or enlarge patterns pages 102–103.

- Cut all the pieces to overall size and sand all surfaces.

- Attach the pattern to the wood, drill all ¼-inch-diameter holes and cut them out.

- Make the base (part No. 7). Notch at "C" for tab the tab (parts No. 1 and 2).

- Cut parts 4, 5A and 5B.

- Put all the pieces together with pins. Do not use glue at this point.

- Glue tabs "C" into the base.

- Stain to suit and add a clear top coat

- Add the movement assembly.

¹⁄₁₆" dia. hole 4 places

③

Enlarge 200%

②

TOP VIEW

⑥

UP

¼" dia. hole
7 places

FRONT VIEW

New England Wall Clock

This simple clock will add a genuine New England flare to any room. It is a simple clock to make. If you don't have equipment to make the frame (part No. 1), most building supply companies have a molding that matches the profile of part No. 1. This project can be stained or painted. The dial face will brighten up the whole room. Any wood can be used; mahogany is used here.

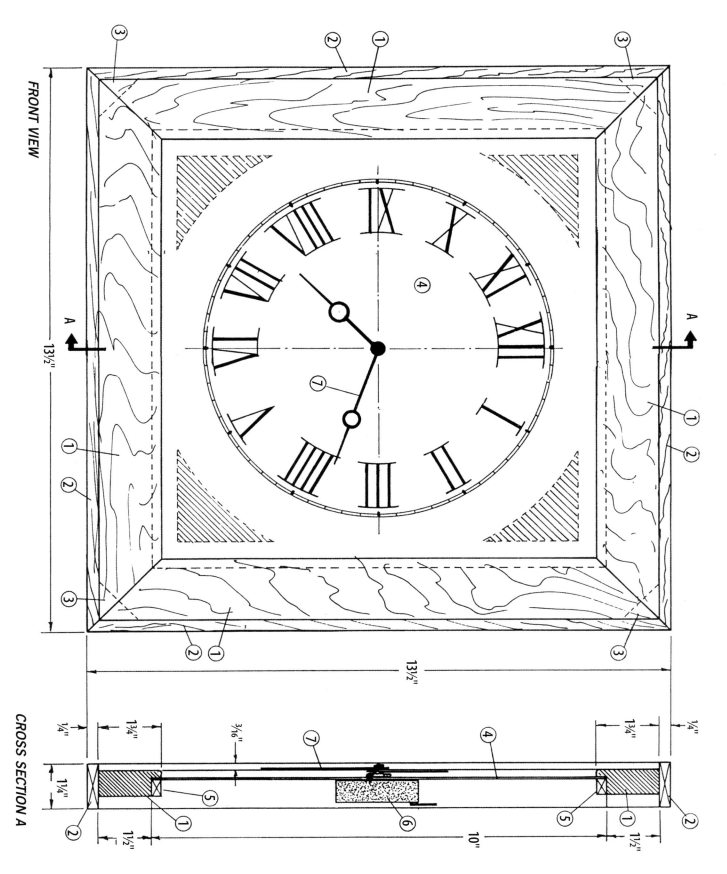

FRONT VIEW

13½"

13½"

A

A

CROSS SECTION A

¼"   1¾"

3/16"

1¼"

1½"   10"

1¾"   ¼"

1½"

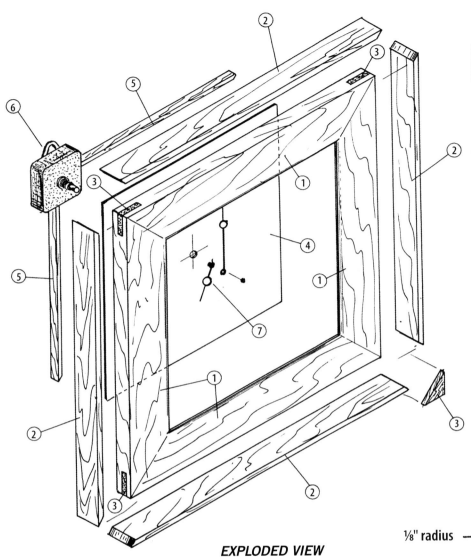

EXPLODED VIEW

- Use the pattern at full size.

- Cut the pieces to size according to the cutting list. Sand all over.

- Use the section view to make the frame piece from ¾" x 1¾" x 72" wood. Make 45-degree cuts, 13 inches long. Glue together.

- Make 45-degree cuts at all four corners for the spline and glue the spline in place.

- Add the trim around the perimeter.

- Sand all over and stain or paint to suit.

- Apply a clear top coat.

- Add the dial. Hold in place with the insert (part No. 5).

- Add the movement with hanger, then add the hands.

No.	Name	Size	Qty
1	Frame	¾" x 1¾" – 13"	4
2	Trim	¼" x 1¼" – 13½"	4
3	Spline	⅛" x ¾" – 1¼"	4
4	Dial face	7½" time ring, metal	1
5	Insert	¼" x ½" – 11"	4
6	Movement	Quartz	1
7	Moon hands	3⅛" size	1 pr

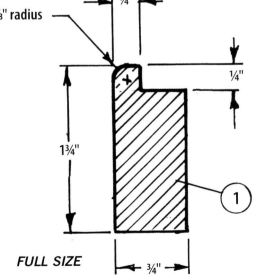

⅛" radius

¼"

¼"

1¾"

¾"

FULL SIZE

FRAME DETAIL (make-up 72")

Simple Schoolhouse Clock

From the turn of the century, Schoolhouse clocks were hung in every class room throughout the country. I can remember sitting in class listening the tick-tock sound, all day. The janitor would come in with a step ladder and wind it once, every week. Today, you can have a taste of these wonderful old clocks. The original Schoolhouse clocks were made of red oak, as is this sample.

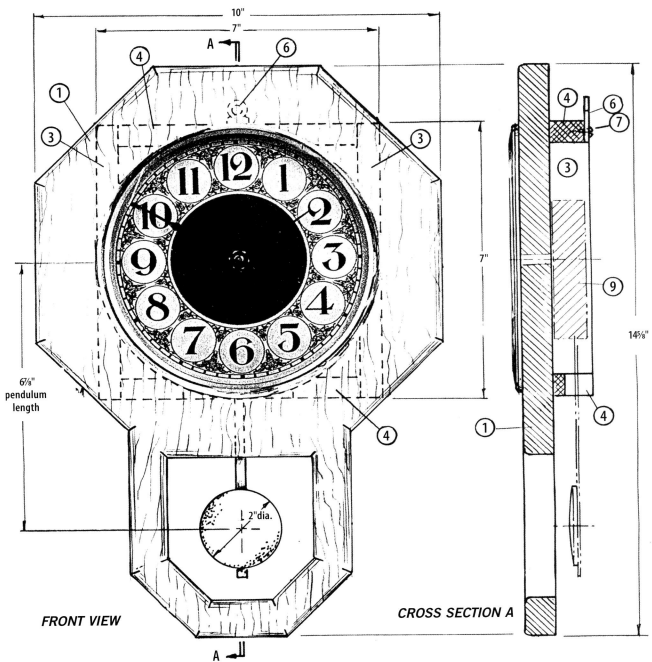

FRONT VIEW

CROSS SECTION A

10"
7"
7"
14⅝"

A

6⅞"
pendulum
length

2"dia.

No.	Name	Size	Qty
1	Front	¾" x 10" – 14⅝"	1
2	Hands	3⅛" size	1 pr.
3	Side	½" x 1" – 7" long	2
4	Top/bottom	½" x 1" – 6" long	2
5	Brad	1" long	12
6	Hanger - brass	To suit	1
7	Screw - round head	As required	2
8	Bezel w. dial face	6¾" dia.	1
9	Movement w/pendulum	6⅞" length	1

Simple Schoolhouse Clock **113**

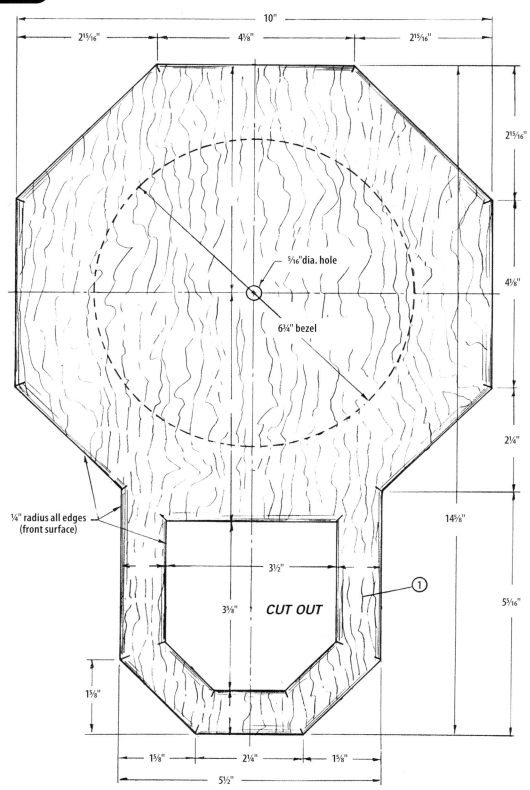

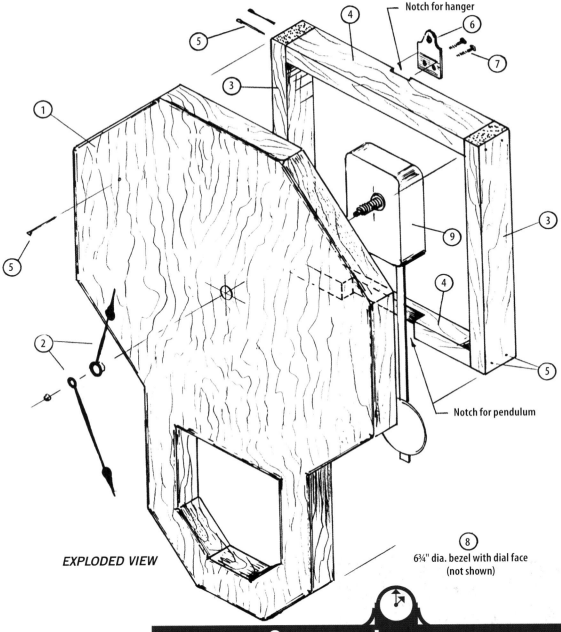

Notch for hanger

Notch for pendulum

EXPLODED VIEW

8
6¾" dia. bezel with dial face
(not shown)

SPECIAL INSTRUCTIONS

- Cut all the pieces to overall size according to the cutting list.
- Use full-size pattern included in this book's envelope, or enlarge pattern on p. 114.
- Layout the front (part No. 1).
- Cut out the front and round all edges using a ¼-inch router bit with a follower.
- Drill a ⁵⁄₁₆-inch-diameter hole.
- Sand all over and stain to suit.

- Make a box from parts No. 3, 4 and 5. Make a notch for the brass hanger (part No. 6) and pendulum.
- Glue box to the back of the front.
- Apply a clear top coat.
- Add the dial/bezel.
- Add the movement with batteries.
- Add the hands.

Country Pantry Clock

This clock is very functional. It will tell you the time and provide shelf space for your favorite collection. It looks great stained or painted. If you paint it, you might want to distress it to give it a worn "country" look. Try to use a hardwood if you can. This one is made from maple.

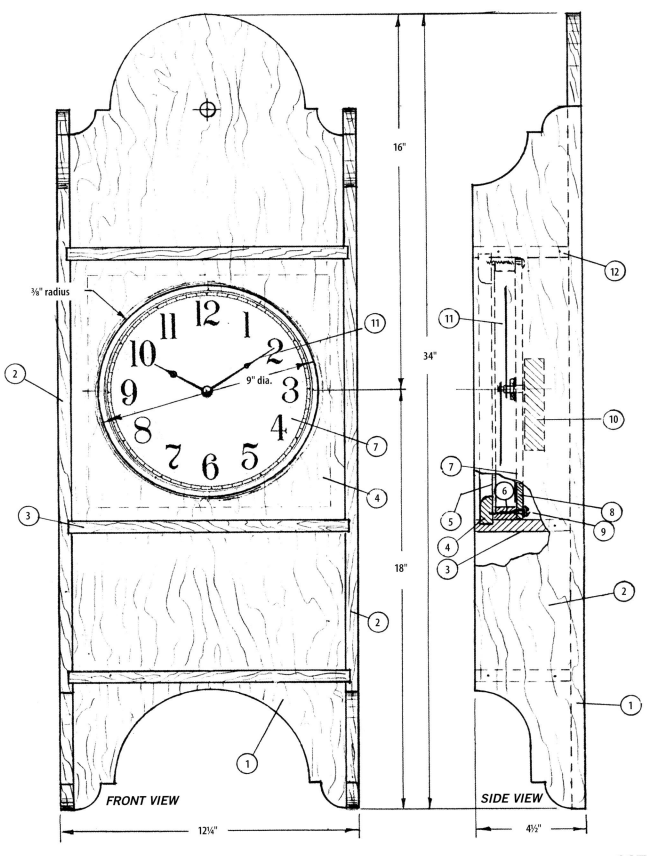

³⁄₈" radius

9" dia.

16"

34"

18"

12¼"

4½"

FRONT VIEW

SIDE VIEW

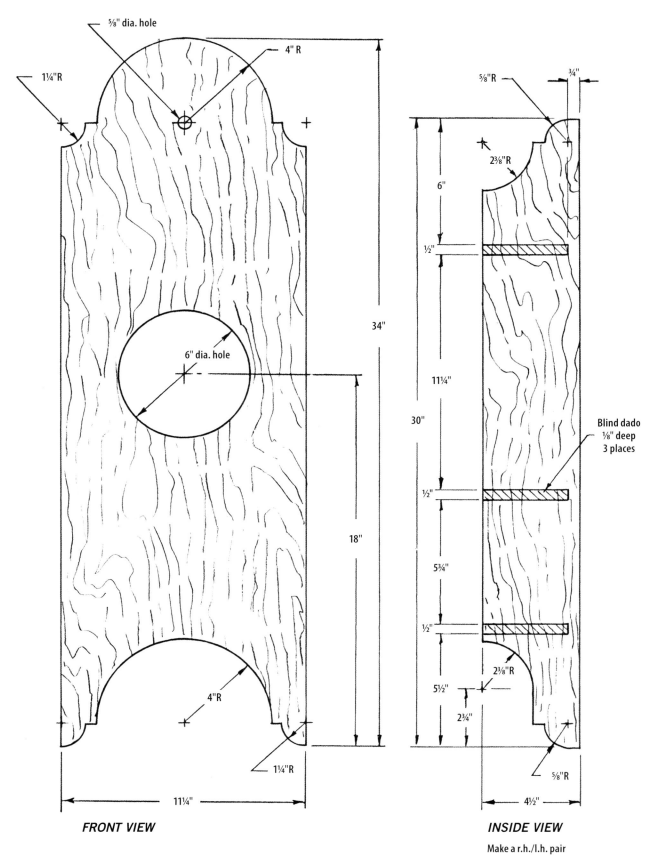

⁵⁄₈" dia. hole

4" R

1¼"R

5⁄8"R

3⁄4"

2⅜"R

6"

½"

5⁄8" dia. hole... 6" dia. hole

34"

30"

11¼"

Blind dado
⅛" deep
3 places

½"

18"

5¾"

½"

4"R

5½"

2⅜"R

2¾"

1¼"R

5⁄8"R

11¼"

4½"

FRONT VIEW

INSIDE VIEW

Make a r.h./l.h. pair

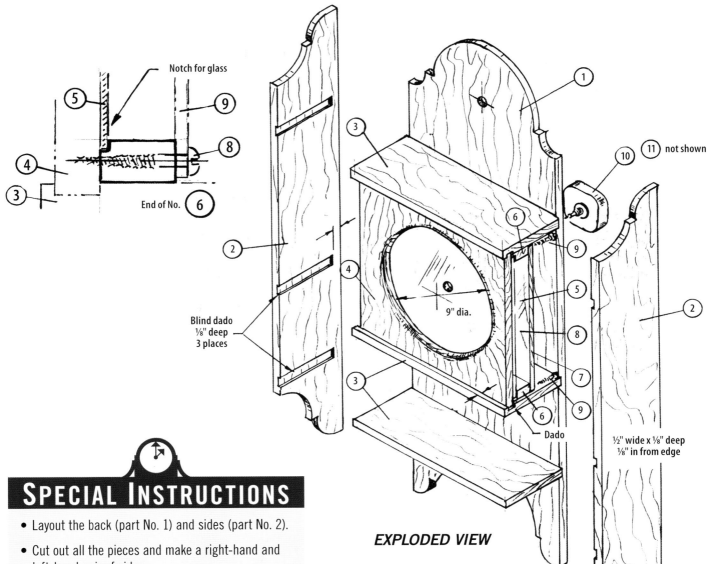

Notch for glass

End of No. (6)

Blind dado
⅛" deep
3 places

9" dia.

Dado

½" wide x ⅛" deep
⅛" in from edge

EXPLODED VIEW

SPECIAL INSTRUCTIONS

- Layout the back (part No. 1) and sides (part No. 2).

- Cut out all the pieces and make a right-hand and left-hand pair of sides.

- Carefully make blind dados in the sides (part No. 2).

- Cut dados in the shelves (part No. 3) as shown in the exploded view.

- Dry fit all the pieces and adjust any, if necessary.

- Sand all the pieces, keeping all edges sharp.

- Stain or paint and apply a clear top coat.

- Add glass, face, movement and hands before assembly.

- Glue all the parts together except the backer (part No. 7). Screw it in place.

No.	Name	Size	Qty
1	Back	½" x 11¼" – 34"	1
2	Side	½" x 4½" – 30"	2
3	Shelf	½" x 4" – 11½"	3
4	Face	½" x 11¼" – 11½"	1
5	Glass	10¾" x – 11⅛"	1
6	Spacer	½" x ⅞" – 11¼"	2
7	Backer	⅛" x 11³⁄₁₆" – 11³⁄₁₆"	1
8	Paper dial	10" size - 8½" time ring	1
9	Screw - rd. hd.	No. 6 – 1¼"	4
10	Movement	Quartz to suit	1
11	Hands	4" length	1 pr.

Collector's Shelf Clock

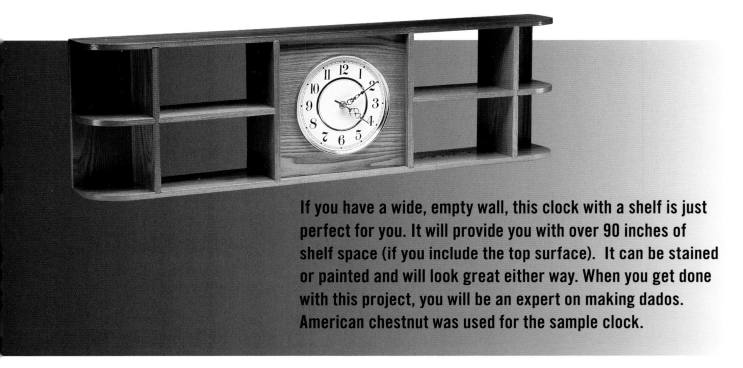

If you have a wide, empty wall, this clock with a shelf is just perfect for you. It will provide you with over 90 inches of shelf space (if you include the top surface). It can be stained or painted and will look great either way. When you get done with this project, you will be an expert on making dados. American chestnut was used for the sample clock.

SPECIAL INSTRUCTIONS

- Make all dados, taking care to make exact 90-degree cuts.
- Round the ends of parts No 1, 6 and 7.
- Dry fit all pieces and trim if necessary.
- Glue all pieces together.
- Sand all over.
- Stain or paint and apply a clear top coat.
- Add the bezel, dial face movement and hands.

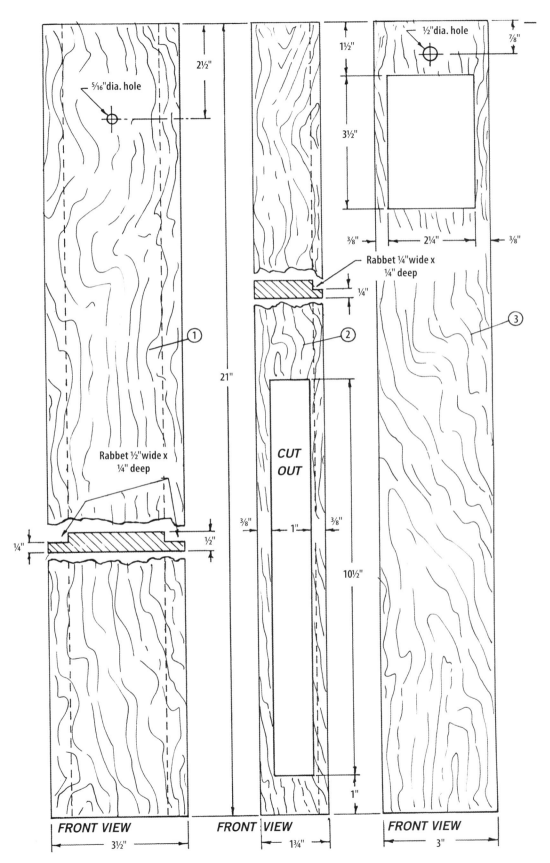

5⁄16"dia. hole

2½"

½"dia. hole

7⁄8"

1½"

3½"

⅜"

2¼"

⅜"

Rabbet ¼"wide x
¼" deep

¼"

①

②

③

Rabbet ½"wide x
¼" deep

¼"

½"

21"

⅜"

1"

⅜"

CUT
OUT

10½"

1"

FRONT VIEW

3½"

FRONT VIEW

1¾"

FRONT VIEW

3"

Krazy Klock

If you want a real challenge and an unusual project—here it is. You will amaze your family and friends and even yourself with this one. Use contrasting wood for each piece. Maple and walnut were used here.

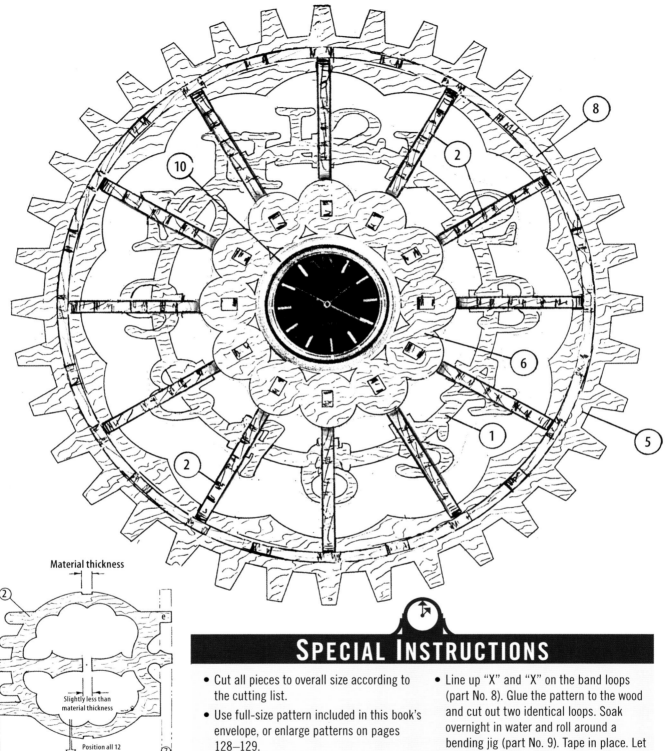

Material thickness

Slightly less than
material thickness

Position all 12
toward center

Center

LOOP
1 req'd

Enlarge 130%

SPECIAL INSTRUCTIONS

- Cut all pieces to overall size according to the cutting list.
- Use full-size pattern included in this book's envelope, or enlarge patterns on pages 128–129.
- Carefully cut out all the pieces. Be sure all the slots are the same width as the thickness of wood.
- Dry fit all the pieces. This will take a little adjusting and fitting as you put it together.

- Line up "X" and "X" on the band loops (part No. 8). Glue the pattern to the wood and cut out two identical loops. Soak overnight in water and roll around a bending jig (part No. 9). Tape in place. Let dry for 48 hours.
- Glue bands (part No. 8) to the outside ring (part No. 5).
- Carefully assemble and apply light glue.
- Add fit up (part No. 10).

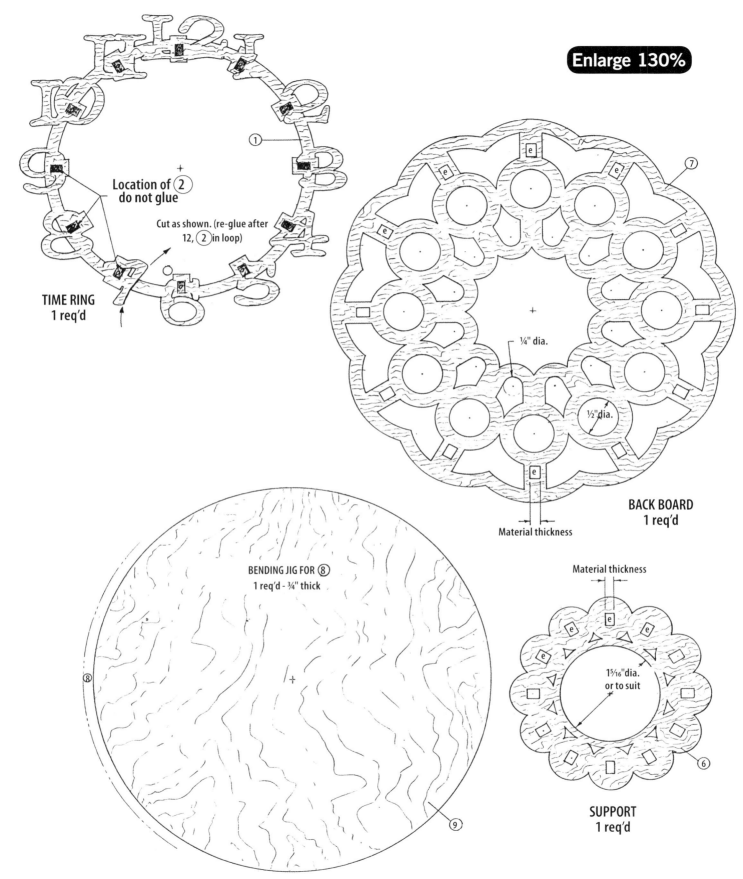

Enlarge 130%

Location of ②
do not glue

Cut as shown. (re-glue after
12, ② in loop)

TIME RING
1 req'd

①

⑦

¼" dia.

½"dia.

e

BACK BOARD
1 req'd

Material thickness

BENDING JIG FOR ⑧
1 req'd - ¾" thick

⑧

⑨

Material thickness

e

1⁵⁄₁₆"dia.
or to suit

⑥

SUPPORT
1 req'd

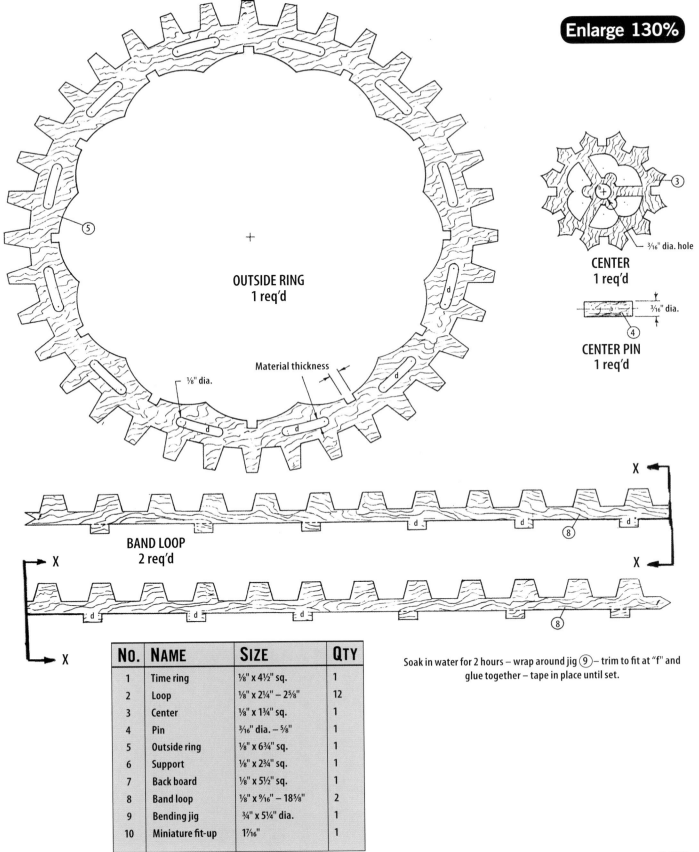

OUTSIDE RING
1 req'd

¹⁄₈" dia.

Material thickness

CENTER
1 req'd

³⁄₁₆" dia. hole

³⁄₁₆" dia.

CENTER PIN
1 req'd

BAND LOOP
2 req'd

X

X

No.	Name	Size	Qty
1	Time ring	¹⁄₈" x 4½" sq.	1
2	Loop	¹⁄₈" x 2¼" – 2⅝"	12
3	Center	¹⁄₈" x 1¾" sq.	1
4	Pin	³⁄₁₆" dia. – ⅝"	1
5	Outside ring	¹⁄₈" x 6¾" sq.	1
6	Support	¹⁄₈" x 2¾" sq.	1
7	Back board	¹⁄₈" x 5½" sq.	1
8	Band loop	¹⁄₈" x ⁹⁄₁₆" – 18⅝"	2
9	Bending jig	¾" x 5¼" dia.	1
10	Miniature fit-up	1⁷⁄₁₆"	1

Soak in water for 2 hours – wrap around jig ⑨ – trim to fit at "f" and glue together – tape in place until set.

Onyx Office Clock

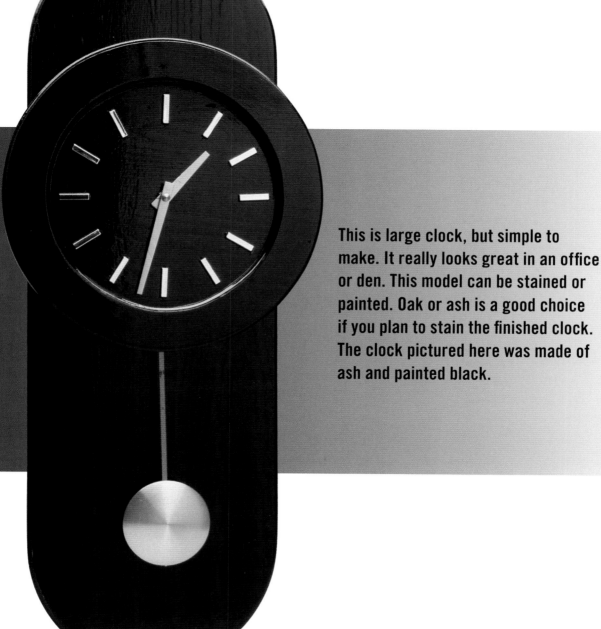

This is large clock, but simple to make. It really looks great in an office or den. This model can be stained or painted. Oak or ash is a good choice if you plan to stain the finished clock. The clock pictured here was made of ash and painted black.

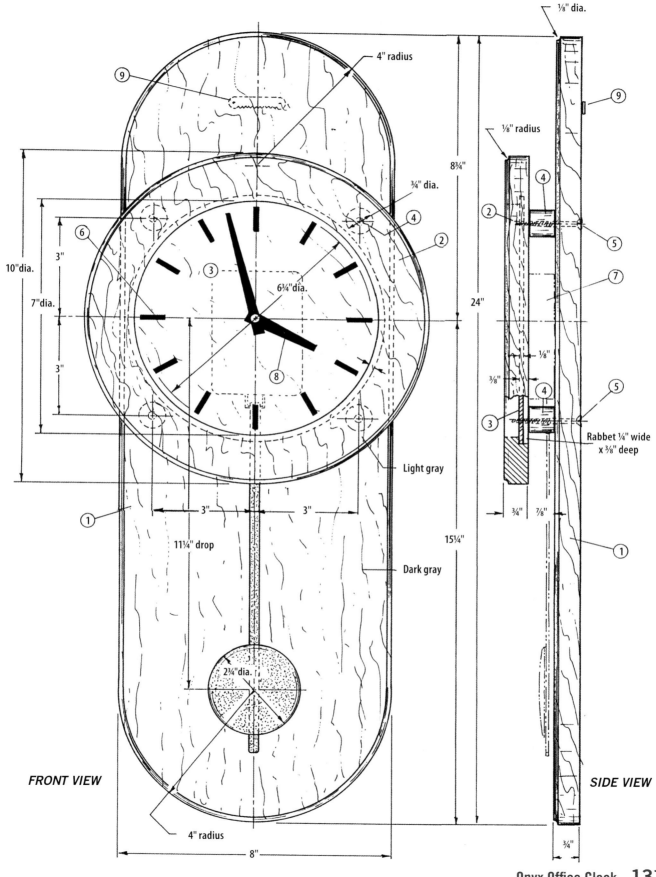

4" radius

⑨

8¾"

¾" dia.

④

②

10"dia.

③

⑥

6¾"dia.

7"dia.

3"

3"

⑧

3"

Light gray

①

3"

3"

11¼" drop

15¼"

Dark gray

2¾"dia.

4" radius

8"

FRONT VIEW

⅛" dia.

⑨

⅛" radius

④

②

24"

⑤

⑦

⅛"

⅜"

④

③

⑤

Rabbet ¼" wide
x ⅜" deep

①

¾"   ⅞"

¾"

SIDE VIEW

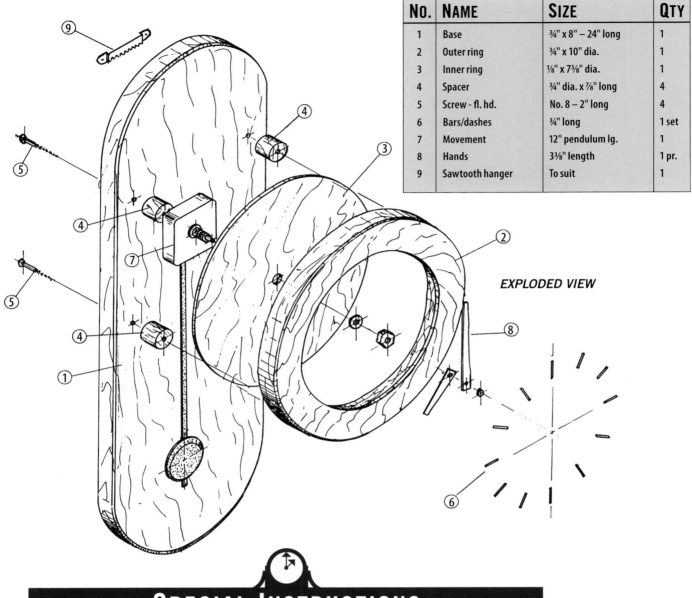

NO.	NAME	SIZE	QTY
1	Base	¾" x 8" – 24" long	1
2	Outer ring	¾" x 10" dia.	1
3	Inner ring	⅛" x 7⅜" dia.	1
4	Spacer	¾" dia. x ⅞" long	4
5	Screw - fl. hd.	No. 8 – 2" long	4
6	Bars/dashes	¾" long	1 set
7	Movement	12" pendulum lg.	1
8	Hands	3⅜" length	1 pr.
9	Sawtooth hanger	To suit	1

EXPLODED VIEW

SPECIAL INSTRUCTIONS

- Layout and cut out the base (part No. 1). Using a ⅛-inch radius with follower, make cut around the outside edge.
- Layout and cut out the outer ring (part No. 2).
- Layout and cut out the inner ring (part No. 3) using a ⅛-inch radius router bit.
- Make the outer ring.
- Sand all the pieces.

- Check the thickness of your clock movement (part No. 7). The spacers (part No. 4) can be lengthened if movement is too thick. (A ⅞-inch-long spacer is shown).
- Stain or paint all pieces.
- Apply a clear top coat.
- Add dashes (part No. 6).
- Assemble all the pieces.
- Add the movement and hands.

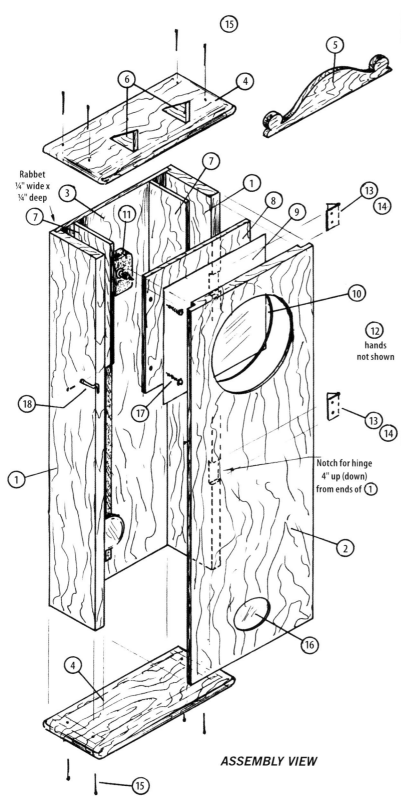

Rabbet
¼" wide x
¼" deep

Notch for hinge
4" up (down)
from ends of ①

12
hands
not shown

ASSEMBLY VIEW

SPECIAL INSTRUCTIONS

- Cut all wood to overall size and sand all over.

- Study the exploded view to see exactly how the clock is put together.

- Make the required rabbet cuts as shown.

- Cut out a 7½-inch-diameter hole for the dial face and an oval-shaped hole.

- Round the edges of the round and oval holes in the door. Rabbet a lip to support the glass.

- Make a box using parts No. 1, 3 and 4.

- Add supports (part No. 7).

- Fit the door to the box and sand all the pieces.

- To make a pattern for part No. 5, simply have an enlarged copy made that is 10½ inches wide.

- Dry fit all the remaining pieces and assemble the clock.

- Apply stain and top coat.

- Add the dial face and movement. (If using a paper dial face, glue it to the backing, part No. 8.)

No.	Name	Size	Qty
1	Side	⅝" x 3¾" – 28½"	2
2	Door	⅝" x 9½" – 28⁷⁄₁₆"	1
3	Back	¼" x 8¾" – 28½"	1
4	Top/bottom	⅜" x 4½" – 11"	2
5	Splat	⅜" x 2¾" – 10½"	1
6	Brace	½" x 1" – 2"	2
7	Support	½" x 2½" – 12½"	2
8	Backing	¼" x 8½" – 8½"	1
9	Dial - paper	7" time ring	1
10	Glass	8" diameter	1
11	Movement w/ pend	20¼" pendulum	1
12	Hands	3½" size	1 pr
13	Hinge	1¼" x 1"	1 pr.
14	Screws	To suit	As req'd
15	Brads	⅞" long	As req'd
16	Glass - oval	2" x 3"	As req'd
17	Screw - rd. hd.	#4 - ¾" lg.	4
18	Latch	Brass	1

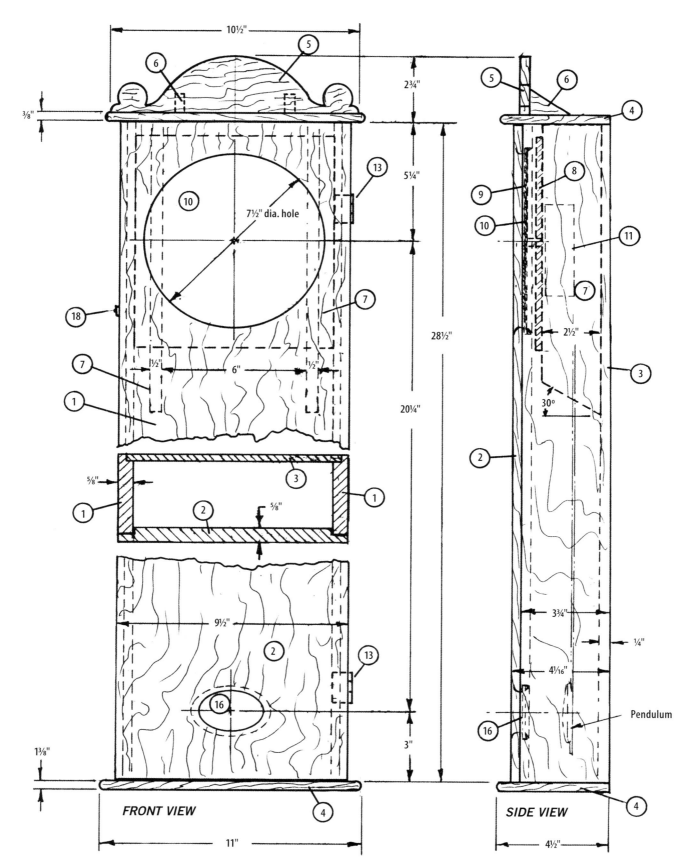

FRONT VIEW

SIDE VIEW

Pendulum

10½"

2¾"

5¼"

28½"

20¼"

3"

1⅜"

11"

3⅛"

7½" dia. hole

1½"

6"

1½"

5⁄8"

5⁄8"

9½"

4½"

2½"

30°

3¾"

¼"

4¹⁄₁₆"

Fancy Cuckoo Clock

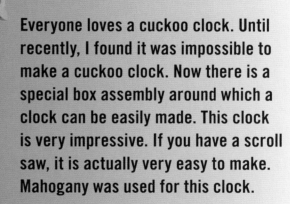

Everyone loves a cuckoo clock. Until recently, I found it was impossible to make a cuckoo clock. Now there is a special box assembly around which a clock can be easily made. This clock is very impressive. If you have a scroll saw, it is actually very easy to make. Mahogany was used for this clock.

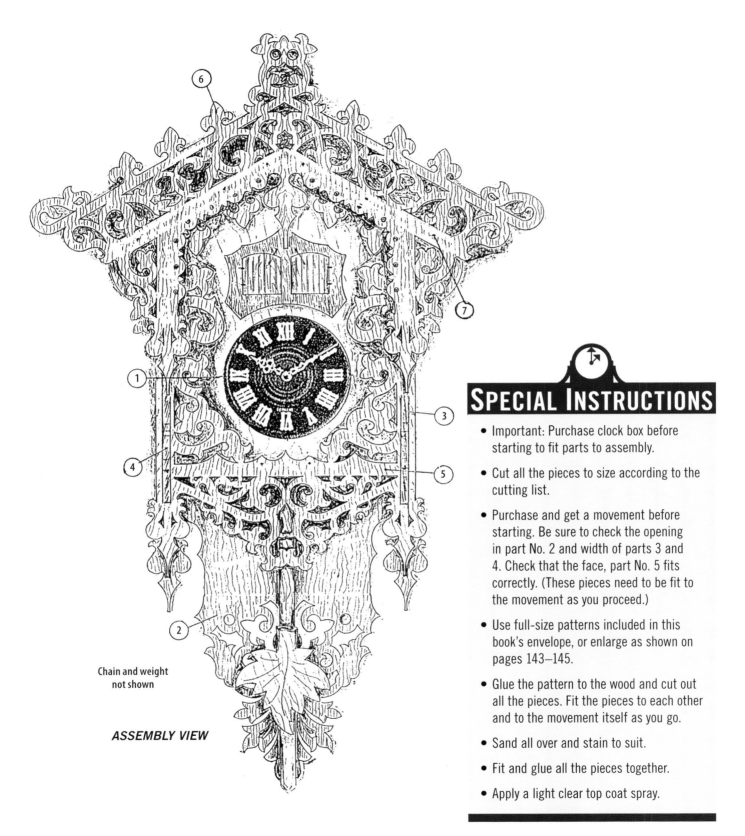

Chain and weight
not shown

ASSEMBLY VIEW

SPECIAL INSTRUCTIONS

- Important: Purchase clock box before starting to fit parts to assembly.

- Cut all the pieces to size according to the cutting list.

- Purchase and get a movement before starting. Be sure to check the opening in part No. 2 and width of parts 3 and 4. Check that the face, part No. 5 fits correctly. (These pieces need to be fit to the movement as you proceed.)

- Use full-size patterns included in this book's envelope, or enlarge as shown on pages 143–145.

- Glue the pattern to the wood and cut out all the pieces. Fit the pieces to each other and to the movement itself as you go.

- Sand all over and stain to suit.

- Fit and glue all the pieces together.

- Apply a light clear top coat spray.

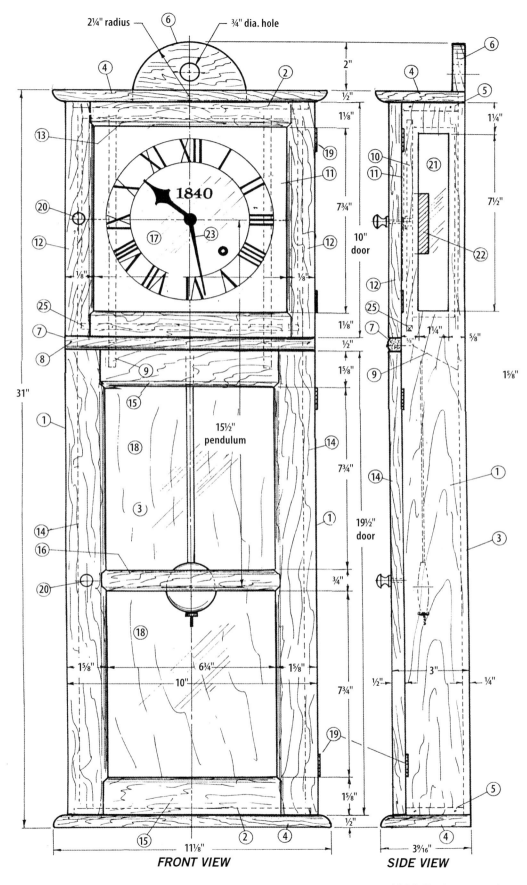

2¼" radius

¾" dia. hole

6

4

2

2"

½"

1⅛"

13

19

11

7¾"

10"
door

20

12

12

1/8"

17

23

1/8"

25

1⅛"

7

½"

8

9

1⅝"

15

31"

1

18

14

3

1

14

16

15½"
pendulum

20

18

1⅝"

6¾"

1⅝"

10"

19½"
door

7¾"

15

2

4

11⅛"

FRONT VIEW

6

4

5

1¼"

10

11

21

7½"

12

22

25

7

⅝"

5/8"

1¼"

9

⅝"

1⅝"

14

1

3

5

½"

3"

¼"

4

3⁹⁄₁₆"

SIDE VIEW

3¾"

19

¾"

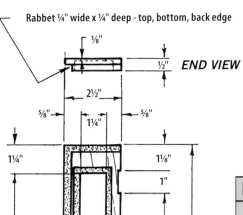

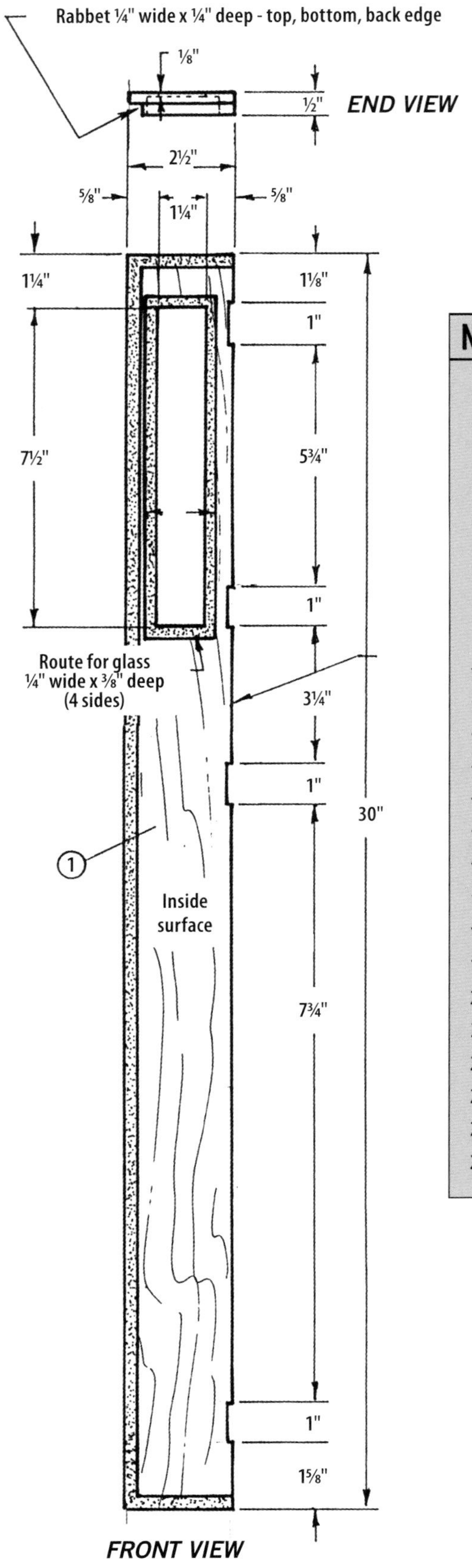

Rabbit ¼" wide x ¼" deep - top, bottom, back edge

⅛"

½"

END VIEW

2½"

⅝"   ⅝"

1¼"

1¼"   1⅛"

1"

7½"   5¾"

1"

Route for glass
¼" wide x ⅜" deep
(4 sides)

3¼"

1"

①

30"

Inside
surface

7¾"

1"

1⅝"

FRONT VIEW

No.	Name	Size	Qty
1	Side	½" x 2½" – 30" long	2
2	Insert	¼" x 2¼" – 9½" long	2
3	Back	¼" x 9½" – 30" long	1
4	Top/Bottom	½" x 3 9/16" – 11⅛" long	2
5	Nail - sq. cut	¾" long (finish)	36
6	Hanger	½" x 2½" – 4½" long	1
7	Divider	½" x ½" – 10" long	1
8	Nail - sq. cut	1" long (finish)	2
9	Dial support	¼" x 1¾" – 13" long	2
10	Dial board	¼" x 8⅞" square	1
11	Dial face	7" time ring	1
12	Stile - upper	½" x 1⅛" – 10" long	2
13	Rail - upper	½" x 1⅛" – 9½" long	2
14	Stile - lower	½" x 1⅝" – 19½" long	2
15	Rail - lower	½" x 1⅝" – 9" long	2
16	Rail - center	½" x ¾" – 8" long	1
17	Glass - upper	3/32" x 8 3/16" square	1
18	Glass - lower	3/32" x 7 3/16" – 8 3/16"	2
19	Hinge (brass)	1" x 1"	4
20	Pull	9/16" dia. x 1¼" long	2
21	Glass - side	3/32" x 1⅝" – 7⅜"	2
22	Movement (15½ to 20" pendulum length)		1
23	Hands, black		1 pr.
24	Magnetic catch	⅜" dia.	2
25	Dial face support	¼" x ¼" – 8⅞"	1

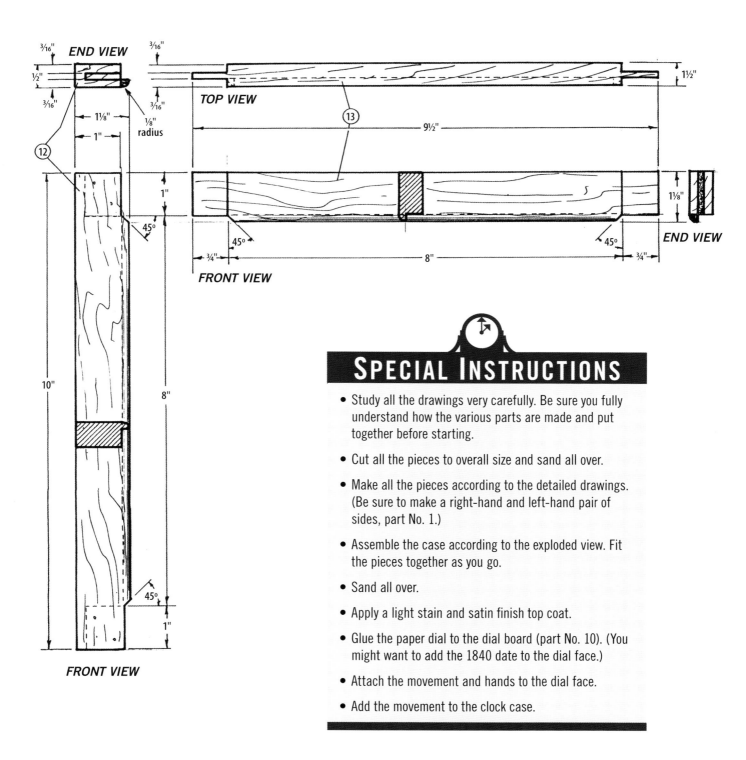

END VIEW

³⁄₁₆"

³⁄₁₆"

½"

³⁄₁₆"

1⅛"

1"

⅛"
radius

12

10"

FRONT VIEW

³⁄₁₆"

TOP VIEW

13

9½"

8"

1"

8"

45°

45°

1"

45°

³⁄₄"

45°

³⁄₄"

FRONT VIEW

1½"

1⅛"

45°

END VIEW

SPECIAL INSTRUCTIONS

- Study all the drawings very carefully. Be sure you fully understand how the various parts are made and put together before starting.

- Cut all the pieces to overall size and sand all over.

- Make all the pieces according to the detailed drawings. (Be sure to make a right-hand and left-hand pair of sides, part No. 1.)

- Assemble the case according to the exploded view. Fit the pieces together as you go.

- Sand all over.

- Apply a light stain and satin finish top coat.

- Glue the paper dial to the dial board (part No. 10). (You might want to add the 1840 date to the dial face.)

- Attach the movement and hands to the dial face.

- Add the movement to the clock case.

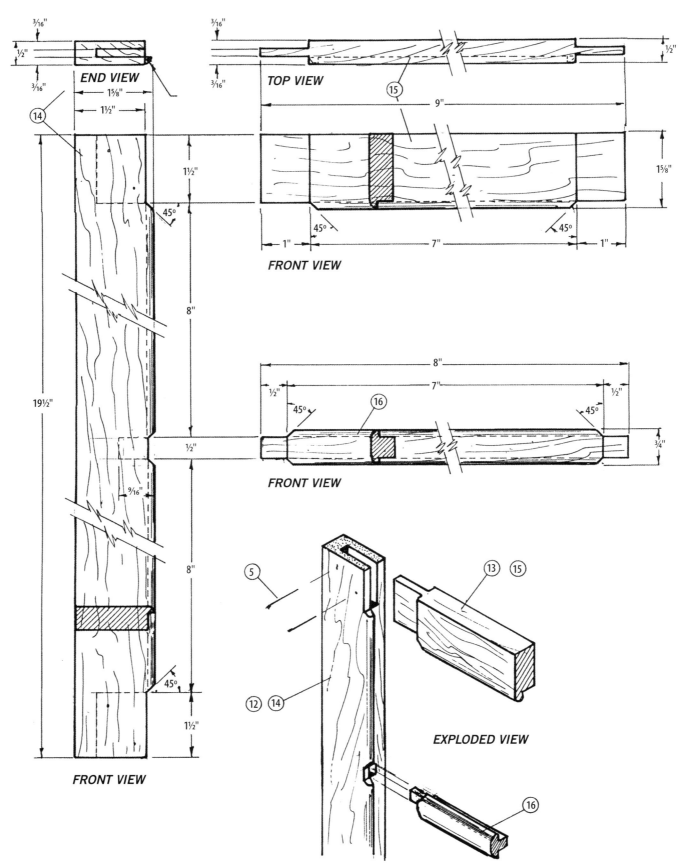

3/16"

1/2"

END VIEW

3/16"

1 5/8"

1 1/2"

(14)

3/16"

TOP VIEW

3/16"

1/2"

(15)

9"

1 5/8"

FRONT VIEW

45°

1 1/2"

45°

45°

1"

7"

1"

19 1/2"

8"

1/2"

9/16"

8"

1/2"

8"

7"

45°

(16)

45°

3/4"

FRONT VIEW

45°

1 1/2"

FRONT VIEW

(5)

(13) (15)

(12) (14)

EXPLODED VIEW

(16)

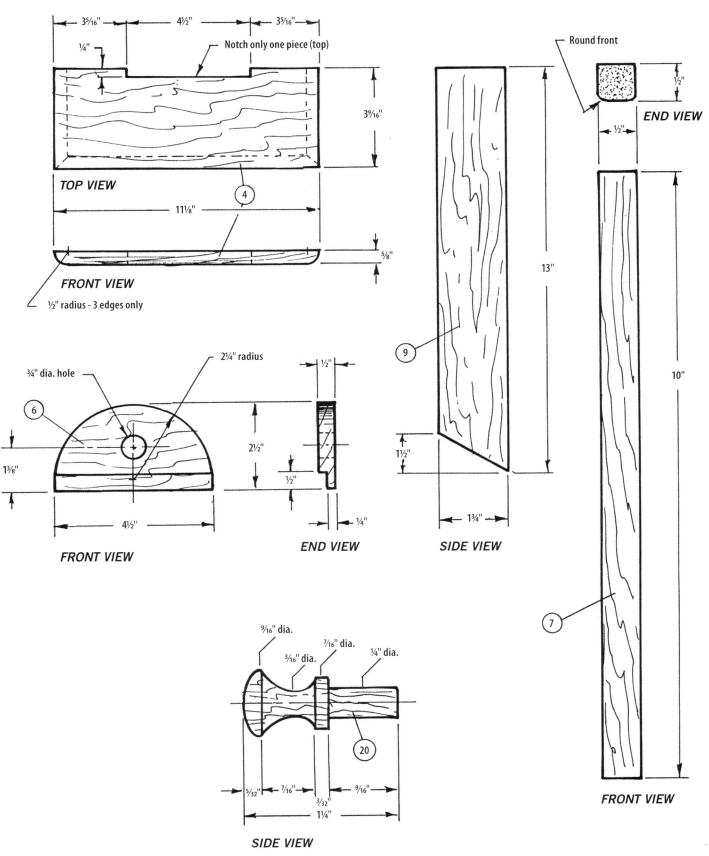

3⁵⁄₁₆" 4½" 3⁵⁄₁₆"

¼" Notch only one piece (top)

3⁹⁄₁₆"

TOP VIEW

④

11⅛"

FRONT VIEW

½" radius - 3 edges only

5⁄8"

Round front

½"

END VIEW

½"

13"

⑨

1½"

1¾"

SIDE VIEW

10"

⑦

FRONT VIEW

¾" dia. hole

2¼" radius

⑥

½"

2½"

1⅜"

½"

¼"

4½"

FRONT VIEW

END VIEW

9⁄16" dia.

3⁄16" dia.

7⁄16" dia.

¼" dia.

⑳

5⁄32" 7⁄16" 3⁄32" 9⁄16"

1¼"

SIDE VIEW

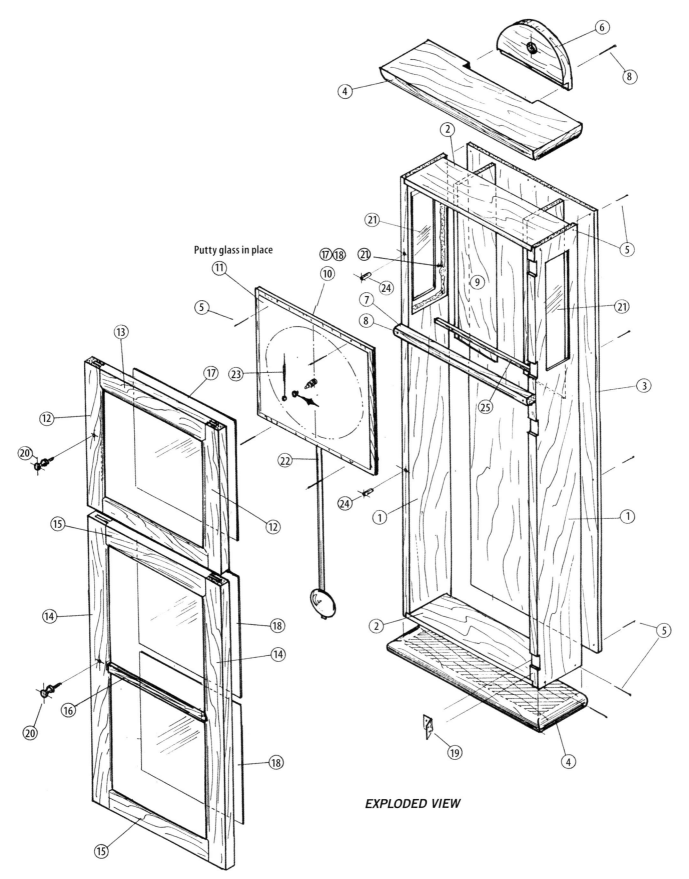

Putty glass in place

EXPLODED VIEW

Appendix B

CLOCK PROJECT WOOD

Common Name	Scientific Name	Description
Afrormosia	*Pericopsis elata*	Exposure darkens the heartwood to a deep orange-brown. Straight to interlocked grain.
Avodire*	*Turraeanthus africanus*	Heartwood is creamy white to pale yellow and darkens to a golden yellow on exposure. Straight but sometimes wavy or interlocking grain.
Butternut	*Juglans cinerea*	Sapwood is white to light grayish-brown; heartwood is light brown, sometimes streaked with dark brown or red. Straight-grained.
Cherry, American	*Prunus serotina*	Sapwood is whitish to reddish-brown; heartwood varies from reddish brown to deep red or light reddish brown. Fine, straight grain.
Chestnut, American	*Castanea dentata*	Heartwood is pale brown with wide growth rings; occasionally "wormy" due to blight.
Cocobolo*	*Dalbergia retusa*	Heartwood color is deep red with yellow, orange, red and even purple streaks. Irregular grain.
Elm, red	*Ulmus hollandica*	Also known as Dutch elm or English elm. Hardwood is brown with distinct annual rings. Straight-grained.
Elm, American white	*Ulmus americana*	Hardwood is medium reddish-brown. Straight, sometimes interlocking
Goncalo Alves*	*Astronium fraxinifolium*	Sapwood is brownish-white; heartwood golden brown to reddish brown with irregular blackish-brown streaks. Wavy or interlocked grain.
Lacewood	*Platanus hybrida*	Heartwood is light reddish-brown with a flecked appearance. Straight-grained.
Mahogany, African*	*Khaya ivorensis*	Heartwood is light to deep reddish-brown. Straight to interlocking grain. Many different varieties exist under the popular name mahogany.
Maple, Sugar or Hard	*Acer saccharum*	Wood is creamy-white with a reddish tinge; heartwood on large trees may be dark brown. Straight-grained.
Mapel, Soft	*Acer rubrum*	Creamy-white wood. Straight-grained, but highly figured when sliced.
Oak, American Red	*Quercus rubra*	Sapwood is whitish to grayish or pale reddish-brown; heartwood is pinkish to light reddish-brown. Straight-grained.
Oak, American White	*Quercus alba*	Color varies from pale yellow-brown to beige with a pinkish tint. Straight-grained.
Pine, Yellow	*Pinus strobus*	Heartwood color varies from a pale straw color to light reddish-brown. Straight-grained.
Poplar, Yellow (Tulip)	*Liriodendron tulipifera*	Sapwood is whitish; heartwood varies from pale yellowish-brown to pale olive brown with darker streaks. Straight-grained.
Purplewood*	*Peltogyne paniculata*	Sapwood is pale red or pink; heartwood darkens to purple upon exposure. Straight-grained.
Satinwood*	*Chlorxylon swietenia*	Heartwood is a golden yellow color, darkening to golden brown with darker streaks. Interlocked and variegated grain.
Walnut	*Juglans nigra*	Heartwood is rich, dark brown. Mostly straight-grained, occasionally wavy or curly.
Zebrawood*	*Microberlinia brazzavillensis*	Heartwood is light golden-yellow with streaks of dark brown or black. Interlocked or wavy grain.

*These woods may have toxic properties. Research them carefully before using them in a clock project.

INDEX

Note: Page numbers in *italics* indicate projects.

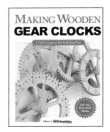

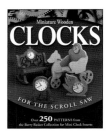